2012 **Marketing Guide** FOR

Stylists • Booth Renters • Independent Salon Owners

The One to Watch

I0472115

2012 Major U.S. Holidays and Observances

January 1	New Years Day (Observed Monday, Jan. 2)
January 16	Martin Luther King Jr. Day
February 14	Valentines Day
February 20	Presidents Day
March 11	Daylight Savings Time Begins
March 17	St. Patricks Day
April 8	Easter Sunday
May 13	Mothers Day
May 28	Memorial Day
June 17	Fathers Day
July 4	Independence Day
September 3	Labor Day
October 8	Columbus Day
October 31	Halloween
November 4	Daylight Savings Time Ends
November 6	Election Day
November 11	Veterans Day (Observed Monday, Nov. 12)
November 22	Thanksgiving
December 24	Christmas Eve
December 25	Christmas Day
December 31	New Years Eve

by **elizabeth kraus**
www.12monthsofmarketing.com
be inpulse branding, marketing and design
author of 365 days of marketing
and make over your marketing:
12 months of marketing for salon and spa

As a stylist, booth renter or independent salon owner, you might not know how important marketing is to your success, whether or not you ever plan to own your own salon or spa.

When you think of the word "marketing" what comes to mind? If you think of things like advertisements, press releases, events, websites and internet marketing, you aren't thinking big enough.

Marketing isn't just for businesses. In a sense, as human beings, we all use marketing tactics in many areas of our lives, because marketing is not about activities you do to promote a business, marketing is about relationships.

Specifically, marketing includes anything that you do to attract, engage, motivate or retain people in relationships; in the case of your professional life, these are relationships with customers.

So 'Marketing' includes *anything* that helps you:

1. attract new customers through referral, because of your reputation, by identifying your 'ideal' type of clients and finding ways to interact with them

2. engage clients to a deeper level of relationship and dependence upon you as their stylist and as their expert resource for hair care and product recommendations

3. motivate clients to take actions you want them to take such as coming to see you more often or for more and different types of services, buying retail products from you, referring their co-workers, friends and family to you or attending events; and,

4. retain clients by developing loyalty, which only occurs when clients truly believe that you care about them, personally, above and beyond the business relationship, and that you put their best interests first.

Some of the activities and tactics that help you do these things are obvious, like using gift cards, special offers, coupons or flyers to tell people about your services.

But some are less obvious. For instance, when you think about the types of clients you most want to attract, do you consider how your personal appearance, interpersonal behaviors, communication skills and other factors work to attract or repel your 'ideal client' types (also known as your target market)?

Do you ensure that your work station is clean and comfortable for each and every client or do you view this as someone else's responsibility? Your clients aren't going to care whose responsibility it is. If something goes wrong while in your care, they will likely view it as your shortcoming.

Do you talk about retail products like a sales person, or do you talk about retail products from a problem-solution, condition-cure point of view? If you aren't recommending retail products to your client, you are not just losing retail sales, you are losing the opportunity to make yourself the expert resource for your client.

And what's worse, say that you don't recommend a product, but the next stylist they see does. They may be led to believe that you either didn't recognize a condition or that you didn't care enough to help them solve the problem.

Take time to step back and examine the experience that most of your customers have when they come to see you. Ask a friend or trusted client to help you look at each step the client takes when they come to see you, from the phone call, text or email to book an appointment, to the appointment itself and through to the end of the appointment.

See how many little things you didn't notice before that could be changed to improve the overall client experience:

- could it be easier to book an appointment?

- how are customers greeted when they arrive? do they have a comfortable place to wait? how long do they typically have to wait? are there beverages and rest rooms for their convenience? do they know where they are?

- have you slacked off when it comes to doing a proper consultation at the beginning of the appointment?

- do you ensure client comfort at the backbar?

- do you see clients all the way to the door or leave them on their own while you move on to the next customer?

- do you thank your clients or follow up after appointments in any way?

There may be dozens of ways to improve the customer experience for your clients with just a little creativity and analysis.

Even though analyzing and improving the client experience makes perfect sense, a little comparison shopping will also show you that few people are taking the time to do it.

Creating a client experience which is truly exceptional and which exceeds the clients typical expectations can make you

the one to watch!

Use this calendar to plan, track and keep your marketing momentum, all year long.

In it, you'll find hundreds of marketing ideas and the inspiration you need to build a bigger role for your business in the lives of your clients. In addition to the ideas, also you'll find visual helpers in each calendar month that are there as a go-by for when you need to do certain tasks:

For instance, when you see [f] this icon, post something on Facebook (at a minimum; you can post more often if you want!)

When you see [t] this icon, that's your reminder to cross-post what you posted on Facebook, your blog, website or email newsletter to Twitter.

Twice each month, you'll see [rss] this icon, your cue to post something on your blog. The Facebook and Twitter icons beside the blog icon should remind you to cross-post a link to your new blog post on both Facebook and Twitter—killing 3 social media 'birds' with one stone!

Whenever you find this icon, [email] send email and/or direct mail communication to your contacts. Since this reminder always falls on the same day as Facebook and Twitter reminders, for social media posts that day, simply cross-post back to your email newsletter. Once again, a 3-for-1 when it comes to completing social media tasks and getting the most out of your marketing toolbox!

You might wonder why **social media (Facebook, Twitter, blogging)** and **email marketing** are **foundational** to your **marketing plan.**

There are two really good reasons for this.

First, they are inexpensive and relative easy to use. Before the advent of the internet, big companies with deep pockets had all the advantages when it came to advertising. The internet changed that.

Now, people don't open the Yellow Pages when it's time to find a new salon or stylist. Instead, they 'Google' or otherwise search the internet. While they might make one trip to their mailbox every day, they make multiple trips to their email inbox. And they are interacting on social media, especially on Facebook.

This brings me to the second reason that social media is foundational to any business-building plan. That's where you'll find your customers.

As of October, 2011, socialmediaexaminer.com said that one out of every 8 minutes spent online is spent on Facebook. HubSpot.com claims that one out of every 6 minutes spent online is spent on social media.

Knowing how to use social media to attract, engage, motivate and retain clients must be foundational to the marketing plan of every independent beauty pro!

Some of the things you might post on Facebook or Twitter, or write about in brief (1-3 paragraphs) blog posts and feature in your emails to clients:

- Links to photos of great styles, current fads and celebrities, fashion icons and trendsetters
- Tips about seasonal scalp and hair care
- Featured product or service of the month (or the week or the day)
- How-to tips for styling at home, how to replicate trends or fads, how to wear trendy accessories like scarves, barrettes or hats, etc.
- Last minute openings on the books
- Changes in hours of operation
- Time-limited product or service promotions
- Event invitations
- Holiday greetings
- Community events, resources and local human interest stories
- Recipes, party, decorating or craft ideas
- Congratulations for local citizen, youth or client accomplishments
- Other types of links or tips which speak to interests that are common among members of your client base

In "The One to Watch" we'll use holidays, observances and themes as the basis to connect, engage and educate your prospects (aka "future clients") and current customers.

January 1 – New Year's Day and January 2 – Remember You Die Day

It's a brand new year and your customers are thinking about all the ways they can improve their lives. They are making New Year Resolutions and right now, they are determined to make the most of every minute. That's what 'Remember You Die Day' is all about!

Use these ideas to bolster your email newsletter, Facebook, Twitter and blog posts:

- Links to sites that can help them meet New Year Resolutions for weight loss and fitness along with ideas, how-to and a New Year Makeover offer that shows them you can get them on the fast-track to looking their best, right now!

- Post motivational, inspirational "seize the day!" type of quotes on Facebook, Twitter and your blog at your station, write or print them on business cards or even use them to create your own personalized bookmarks, cards or notes to give to clients.

  Here's one to get you started:
  "The difference between being a dreamer and someone whose dreams come true is what you do when you're awake." (Elizabeth Kraus) Or you can find more on my website at www.12monthsofmarketing.net/quotes.html.

- Get personal: Write a blog post that tells the story of why you became a stylist and how much you love "what you do." Talk about the difference that you want to make in your client's lives (this is your reason for professional existence!) and share it on your blog, then link to it via Facebook and Twitter.

January 5 – Trivia Day

Use interesting trivia to start conversations or provoke responses on Facebook and Twitter about subjects that would most interest your clients and those types of clients you most want to attract (aka your 'target market').

Hold a Trivia Question of the Day (week or month) contest and reward winner(s) with a product sample, travel or full size retail product or a gift card.

January 11 – Splash a Friend Day

- Splash staff and customers alike with sunshine, kindness, joy, love and optimism. Treat clients to something that will make them smile, maybe by doing something fun, silly or unexpected at the cash register— like how big box warehouse stores punctuate your visit with a big smiley face on your receipt. Think of a way to splash your customers with a little something good just before they leave.

- Sample products customers haven't tried before. Set up a display where they can touch, smell, feel or otherwise experience a new product. Create a mini or appetizer-sized version of a new service to sell or give to customers as your version of a gift-with-purchase.

January 19 – Get to Know Your Customers Day

This may be one of the most important marketing lessons you can learn. To convince people to do business with you, talk about **them**, not yourself. Many people mistakenly believe that marketing means talking about their own skills, products or businesses—**not true!**

Great marketing creates **emotional** **connections** with people because it focuses on **their problems** (and the **solutions** you can provide). Focus your marketing and selling techniques on **connecting** with customers; you want them to know that you **understand** their problems, their concerns, their conditions and **where they are coming from**.

When they feel that you **truly understand** and **relate** to them, they will **trust** you—enough to take you up on recommendations for products and services, and enough to refer friends and family to you as new clients.

Here are some ways you can get to know your customers so that you can **establish emotional connections:**

- Maybe the most obvious way: Ask for their feedback. Take short surveys at the point of sale, on Facebook or by way of follow up email or postcard after an appointment.

- Use polls and surveys to find out what your customers are most interested in (this may or may not even be related to your professional services).

- Use your customer demographic data to understand where most of your clients live, whether they have children, pets, what they do for a living or how they spend their free time.

 Facebook   Twitter   Blog  Email/Mail

January

Sunday	Monday	Tuesday	Wednesday	Thursday	Friday	Saturday
1 **New Years Day** Take/break down expired promotions; set up for January	**2** **Remember You Die Day** **New Years Day** (Observed)	**3** ✉ f t Send January email newsletter and offers	**4**	**5** **Trivia Day**	**6** f t	**7**
8	**9**	**10** f t Begin promoting for Valentine's Day (Tuesday, Feb. 14)	**11** **Splash a Friend Day**	**12**	**13** 🔶 f t	**14**
15	**16** Martin Luther King Jr. Day	**17** f t Look ahead! Finish February details and plan March and April	**18**	**19** f t **Get to Know Your Customers Day**	**20**	**21**
22	**23**	**24** ✉ f t Email / Mail January 'Last Chance!' and Feb/Jan preview	**25**	**26** 🔶 f t	**27**	**28**
29	**30**	**31** f t Take/break down expired promotions; set up for February		**Let the beauty we love be what we do.** (Jalal-Uddin Rumi)		

score card

Check one box for every communication task completed from the above calendar this month:

week one
☐ ☐ ☐ ☐ ☐

week two
☐ ☐ ☐ ☐ ☐

week three
☐ ☐ ☐ ☐

week four
☐ ☐ ☐ ☐ ☐ ☐

week five
☐ ☐

_____# of **New Clients**
Up/Down from last month #_____

_____# of **Retail Products** sold
Up/Down from last month #_____

f _____# of Facebook Fans/Friends
Up/Down from last month #_____

t _____# of Twitter Followers
Up/Down from last month #_____

🔶 _____# of Blog Hits/Readers
Up/Down from last month #_____

✉ _____# of Email Subscribers
Up/Down from last month #_____

_____# of Email Opens (if known)
Up/Down from last month #_____

plan ahead

One class, seminar or webinar you'll attend in the next 2 months:

_____

One technique or technical skill you will improve or master next month:

_____

One thing you resolve to change in your work or personal life next month:

_____

_____

Get Fans, Friends and Followers

Making connections on social media is **easy** when you know how.

And when you do it right you will get the added benefit of adding more of your target audience to your news and post streams. To make connections:

- **Do your clients even know you're there?** Put the link for your Facebook page, Twitter profile, blog site and email subscription form on your business card, or have a special social media business card made just for this. Give this card away to every client in pairs (one to give away).

- Put a "**Like Me** on Facebook" (or "**Follow Me** on Twitter") **sign** at your **station** or by the **cash register**. There are free, ready to use signs on the resources page at www.12monthsofmarketing.net

- Ask friends, family and co-workers to suggest that **their** social media **friends** and followers connect with you online.

- **Post** interesting **content**, photos and quotes – the same kinds of things you yourself like to 'share' with your friends and fans when you see it on other pages.

- **Be present!** Make sure you update your social media profiles often enough to show regular signs of life!

- **Be positive.** Research shows that people who are generally **positive** have far **more followers** and their posts get shared far more often than those who use social media as a forum for complaining or negativity. In fact, positive comments and quotes are the 2nd most **shared item** among Facebook followers!

- Ask your clients to post about the **products and services they** love most. Why? **70%** of Facebook users say that positive referrals from friends make a positive impact on their **buying decisions.**

Did you know?

As of September 2011, the average post on Facebook has a lifespan of less than 24 hours. Here are some more tips for using Facebook as a professional, especially when you are using your personal page for professional use as well:

- Choose **one picture** to use on **all** your social media profiles. This consistency will help followers and peers identify that it's "you," thus helping you build influence as an expert in your field.

- It's called social media – people expect you to **be social and personal first and foremost.** But as in all public media, put your best face forward! Don't post photos or stories you wouldn't want your employer, grandmother, minister or favorite mentor to see.

- **Avoid** profanity, politics, religion and off-color posts; they might make you the one to watch in ways you don't want to be seen.

- **Brush up** on your spelling, grammar and punctuation. Part of being perceived as an expert in your field is in your **presentation.** Here are some of the most common spelling errors people make:

  Lose (opposite of win) vs. Loose (not tight)

  Weird (not wierd)

  Their (possessive, as in, belongs to them) vs. They're (contraction of the 2 words they are) vs. There (a place or idea, as in, go over there)

  Your (possessive, like, that is your hat) vs. You're (a contraction of the 2 words you are)

  It's (a contraction of the 2 words it is) vs. Its (possessive, like, the dog wagged its tail)

  Effect (usually a noun, like, the effect you have on other people) vs. Affect (a verb, like, how your behavior affects other people)

  Weather (snow, rain, sun, etc.) vs. Whether (an either-or statement, such as, I wear my sunglasses, whether it's sunny or not!)

  A lot (ALWAYS 2 words, 'alot' is not a word)

  Then (used for time, like, we'll see the movie, then we'll go to the store) vs. Than (used for comparison, often with more than, better than, less than, worse than, etc.)

Use Current Fashion and Styling Trends

Every month, **find pictures** that show current hair, makeup or styling trends:

- Practice creating current trends and styles (ask a co-worker, friend or family member to help) and take before and after pictures to show your clients.

- Post a link to a picture of a current styling trend each week on Facebook and Twitter, inviting clients to make an appointment to find out how you can help them get this look themselves.

- Write a blog post featuring one of the pictures along with step-by-steps for your customers on how to create the look for themselves, noting the services, haircolor, etc., they need from you to replicate the current trend.

- Be the expert resource for your clients. Keep track of what's coming next in hair, nails and/or makeup and write social media posts that highlight current fads, fashion and trends.

- Ask questions like "who wore it best?" and compare celebrities who are both sporting the same hair or makeup styles.

- Take polls to find out what current hair and makeup trends your customers like most.

- Hold an online contest and reward one person who commented on, liked or shared a Facebook post or 'retweeted' your Twitter post to a free product (such as a product needed to recreate a current style trend) or a gift card they can use toward their trend makeover.

Marketing 101

Effective marketing speaks to customer needs and wants. When you're talking about yourself, you're more likely to be thinking about what **you** need and want (customers and sales) vs. what **your customers** and prospects truly need and want.

Take time to make a list of the things that your customers most need and want (this may require that you do some market research) that your business provides:

- what problems do they have that you have the ability to solve: dry scalp? frizzy hair? limp? won't hold a curl? too much curl? too much or too little volume? graying? thinning?

- what do they desire that your business provides: fashion, style, color, makeup or styling how-to, etc?

- what do they value in their customer experiences?

Your marketing should show that you understand of the needs and wants **of your customers** – make them feel like you're all "in the same boat," so to speak.

Once you have their attention and you've shown them that you understand what they really want and need, then point out how you can meet those wants and needs.

Don't talk about your business or your own personal amazing-ness; instead, focus on the **benefits the customer** can expect as a result of using your products or services, and as a result of doing business with you.

Use holidays, observances and themes as the basis to connect, engage and educate your prospects (aka "future clients") and current customers.

February is Plant the Seeds of Greatness Month

A few years ago I had the honor of attending a private reception with a beauty industry icon; a man whose resume includes dynasties built not just on one but on two continents, the epitome of someone who is **the one to watch.**

He was addressing a room of young cosmetology school student stylists. Instead of talking about any number of his own accomplishments, he stood facing them and said, "How many of you want to be salon owners?" Most raised their hands and he challenged them to **write down their dreams and start working on their business plan now;** telling them that they should start immediately working toward becoming all that they dream of being. That they should not let anyone tell them they weren't good enough, educated enough or smart enough to achieve their dreams.

He told of the challenges he himself had faced during his career and told the group not to let anything hold them back, that there are no excuses and no real obstacles except those we let hold us back.

Hearing the story of someone who didn't let anything stand in his way, I felt all of my own insecurities and excuses fade away and resolved that I was not going to feel inferior to others or inferior to the challenge of pursuing my own dreams any more.

That's what Planting the Seeds of Greatness is about. Yes, it's about gaining real education and experience you need to move to the next level, but it's also about **believing in yourself** and **being bold enough** to take the next step, whatever that is, toward your long term professional and personal goals.

Planting the seeds of greatness is about **defining** and **envisioning** the person that **you want to be** and then **setting out** to become that person.

February 2 - Groundhog Day

Use Groundhog Day Trivia to fuel your social media posts. Hold a contest on Facebook or Twitter asking clients to predict the weather over the next 6 weeks (or for a week or a specific day, etc.) and reward winner/s with product samples or trial sizes or with free add-ons at appointments like scalp massages, deep conditioning, mini manicure, etc.

February 8 - Man Day

Create a "Man's Wish List" of suggested services and products for women to buy as gifts for men's birthdays, Valentine's Day, anniversaries and other special occasions. Create bundled gift sets of men's products or sell a series of services at a special price (such as 3, 6 or 12 men's haircuts) to be used within a given period of time to help fill up your books and ensure desired frequency of visits.

February 12-18 - Flirting Week and February 14 - Valentine's Day

- Post flirting tips or solicit customers flirting ideas and stories on Facebook.

- Suggest products or services (you sell) that could be used to give as a gift to a special someone on Valentine's Day, or which could be sent as a flirtatious gift, such as a kissable lipstick color or a shampoo that makes your hair smell delicious.

- All month, post statements about how much you love your clients and why you love being a stylist on social media and your email newsletter.

- Send a special Valentine's Day email greeting to your contacts.

February 16 - Satisfied Single Day

With all the hoopla about couples, love and Valentines this month, singles in your client base might need some love of their own:

- Educate clients about 'singly satisfying' products and services (such as deep conditioning treatments, all-over haircolor, straightening or texture services, etc.) and communicate their benefits (i.e., how they "satisfy" the customer all on their own).

- Create $1 add-on promotions called "singles" such as a conditioning treatment, scalp massage, gloss finish, styling product with purchase, etc.

February

Sunday	Monday	Tuesday	Wednesday	Thursday	Friday	Saturday
		February is Plant the Seeds of Greatness Month	1 Send February email newsletter and offer	2 **Groundhog Day**	3	4
5	6	7	8 **Man Day**	9	10	11
12	13 **Flirting Week Feb. 12-18**	14 **Valentines Day** Send Valentine's e-greeting	15 Look ahead! Finalize March details and plan April and May	16 **Satisfied Single Day**	17	18
19	20 **Presidents Day Holiday** (Observed)	21 Send email: February 'Last Chance!' and Mar/Apr preview	22	23	24	25
26	27	28	29 **Leap Day**	Take/break down expired promotions; set up for March	**You have to expect things of yourself before you can do them.** (Michael Jordan)	

score card

Check one box for every communication task completed from the above calendar this month:

week one
☐ ☐ ☐ ☐ ☐

week two
☐ ☐ ☐ ☐ ☐

week three
☐ ☐ ☐ ☐ ☐

week four
☐ ☐ ☐ ☐ ☐

week five
☐ ☐

_____ # of **New Clients**
Up/Down from last month #_____

_____ # of **Retail Products** sold
Up/Down from last month #_____

_____ # of Facebook Fans/Friends
Up/Down from last month #_____

_____ # of Twitter Followers
Up/Down from last month #_____

_____ # of Blog Hits/Readers
Up/Down from last month #_____

_____ # of Email Subscribers
Up/Down from last month #_____

_____ # of Email Opens (if known)
Up/Down from last month #_____

plan ahead

One class, seminar or webinar you'll attend in the next 2 months:

_____

One technique or technical skill you will improve or master next month:

_____

One thing you resolve to change in your work or personal life next month:

_____

_____

The One to Watch

Have you ever known someone who seemed to have it all together—who regularly **outperforms** those around them? It's not by accident that they have become **'the one to watch'** themselves, it's on purpose. They don't expend energy on negative behaviors. They focus on the future and on others, rather than themselves.

Here are some behaviors you can choose to **embrace** today that will help you become like that:

- **Develop a personal brand.**

  Your own personal style is reflected in the words you choose to use, the clothes you choose to wear and the detail that you show in your personal appearance.

  Your personal style should be unique and reflect your own tastes, but it should also be a style which contributes to your social and professional success.

- **Don't toe the line.**

  Many times people do no more than what is asked and expected. They toe the line when it comes to how they behave in the workplace, whether they conform to standards of dress and the level at which they work to meet sales and performance goals.

  If you toe the line you will be watched, but for all the wrong reasons.

  Exceed expectations and goals.

  Don't take the "it's not my job" attitude; if you see something that needs to be done, do it.

  Dress for the job that you want, rather than the one that you have.

  Don't knowingly violate the employment policies in place at your salon, even if you don't agree with them. Work to make change the right way.

  Arrive early and put all of the time in that you are expected to.

- **Hold yourself to high standards.**

  Steer clear of gossip and those who gossip. Don't engage in negative conversations about your employer or co-workers.

  Be supportive of the initiatives and programs introduced by your boss (or the salon owner). Do all that you can to see that they are successful. Participate. Encourage.

  Say nice things behind people's backs as well as to their faces. Be generous with sincere compliments to co-workers and clients.

  If you do have criticisms or suggestions for the salon owner, meet with them privately and do your best to express your opinions or suggestions in a calm, clear manner. Use logic and persuasion to help make your point, rather than emotion.

- **Be absolutely present with each client.**

  Each client should feel that they have your full attention while in your care.

  Don't skimp on the consultation, even with clients you feel very comfortable with.

  Don't stop telling clients about conditions you observe in their hair, scalp, skin or nails.

  Don't stop making professional service and product recommendations.

- **Know when to quit.**

  As a stylist, you'll find the stereotype to be true: clients really will tell you everything. Listen, sympathize and let them know that you care and about ways in which you can relate, or empathize with them. But at the end of the day, let go.

  Write a personal note (or an email) of sympathy or encouragement to those who particularly need it.

  At the end of your work day, spend 15 minutes stretching, doing yoga, walking around the block or develop another ritual that will give you an opportunity to release yourself from the cares shared with you that day.

What's love got to do with it?

If you believe your customers need, want and love your services more than you need, want and love them, you're in trouble. You're just a hop, skip and a jump from complacency, neglect or even the condescending disdain that will reveal just how fragile that customer relationship was.

By nearly any measure, you can't support the claim that your customers love you. To understand why, you have to know what characterizes true love:

Love is unselfish and patient. It is slow to take offense and overlooks shortcomings. Love puts the interests of what it loves ahead of its own interests. Those who truly love are almost unconditionally faithful to the object of their affection.

If this describes how your customers feel about you, I want to know where you live and I want to know how I can get some for myself!

The truth is, customers are self-centered.

- They are in the relationship for what they are getting out of it—why *shouldn't* they be?
- They are likely to take offense and notice shortcomings.
- If their interests change, they will go elsewhere. And they are fickle.
- Most are open to the possibility of being wooed by another offer—many people welcome any chance to try something new.

It's like your customers are sitting at the bar, made up, looking hot—just waiting for someone else to buy them a drink.

There is a way to get customer love, but it's going to cost you because your customers are **never** going to put more into the relationship than **you** do.

Imagine a still pool of water providing a reflection. The reflection on the water may be a fair image of the original, but the original is still by far the strongest, clearest side.

Like it or not, the "love" bestowed on you by your clients is a **direct reflection** of your dedication to, engagement with, and interest in, them.

February Extras

The love you show for the customer is the original, their response is the reflection. Just as with the clear pool of water, the reflection is never going to be stronger than the original!

Just as in other relationships, there are some ways to gain and nurture mutual affection:

- Remember the fickle nature of the customer's love and stay on top of your game.
- Deliver expectation-exceeding experiences, every time.
- Be intriguing, engaging and provocative.
- Keep your eyes and ears open for signs of discontent.
- Communicate. Solicit feedback.
- Listen. No, I mean *really* listen.
- Respond to complaints, wants and needs.
- Be open to change. Ask how you can change. When your customer tells you that you need to change, by all means, change!
- Get help from peers when you need it.
- And maybe most importantly: establish emotional connections – give people reasons to love you.

Tell people why you're passionate about 'what you do.' Talk about your connections to the community. Align yourself with a local cause and give back.

It's never about you, it's always about them (your customers).

Don't fall for the lie that your customers love you, or that they need you even close to as much as you need them.

Instead, stay focused on providing benefits and value to your customers, and focus your marketing on telling customers about how doing business with you makes their lives better.

Use holidays, observances and themes as the basis to connect, engage and educate your prospects (aka "future clients") and current customers.

March is Employee Spirit Month

As a stylist, booth renter or independent salon owner, the phrase 'employee spirit month' may not seem like it relates to you, but it does.

In any business, the employee culture — the attitude and consequent behaviors demonstrated everyday in the workplace — has a **profound effect** on the success of the business and its profitability.

Even though you can only control your own attitude and behaviors, the overall employee culture at your salon or spa still impacts your **profitability** and your ability to **attract and retain clients.**

Whether or not it seems fair, it's a dynamic you have to work with. You may have very limited ability to change the overall culture at your workplace, especially if there is no support from management for changing the employee culture.

But you can still impact and improve the attitudes and behaviors of others by **leading through example**. You can bring your best self to work in order to provide your clients with a great experience.

Recognize the **power** your outlook alone has to change the way you approach the day, change the way you interact with co-workers, change the way you feel about your job and especially how your outlook changes the level of service you provide to your clients.

> You cannot control what happens to you, but you can **control your attitude** toward what happens to you, and in that, you will be **mastering change** rather than allowing it to master you.
>
> (Brian Tracy)

March 3 – Unique Names Day

- Hold a contest to determine which of your customers has the most unique name provable by driver's license or birth certificate.

- Ask customers to help rename one or more of your services with unique names or with names that rhyme, are slang, are made-up words, etc. Use entries to 'rename' a different product or service each month as part of a product/service of the month spotlight.

March 8 – Working Women's Day

Collect business cards, emails, Facebook comments or Twitter retweets from working women in your community and hold a drawing, rewarding one of them with a gift card, complimentary service or all-out day of pampering. This is a great way to build your email contact database and your social media following. As you build your following or your email list, you can then send out email newsletters and posts to promote your services, extend new client and referral offers, fill last minute openings, etc.

March 15 – Consumer Rights Day

- Write your own list of guarantees—promises you make to your clients about what will be true each and every time they do business with you. Post these promises at your station, on your Facebook page, as a series of Tweets and include them in your email newsletter.

- Work with your salon owner (or lead the way) in developing a list of guarantees that all of the staff at your business will make to customers. Post these as 'consumer rights' at every employee station, giving credit to each stylist who contributed and promised to uphold them.

March 16 – Lips Appreciation Day

- If you are allowed to sell your own retail, purchase a fun, provocative, themed, or otherwise impulse-buy-stimulating lipstick display for your station to bolster your retail sales. Don't forget other lip-enhancers as well like lip balms, gloss and plumpers.

- Whether it's from your own display or the retail sold in-salon, hold a perfect lips makeup demonstration for clients as a quick, free add-on to appointments; or, working with co-workers, set a date and hold a makeup how-to workshop event for working women, teen or tween clients.

 Facebook  Twitter   Blog  Email/Mail

March

Sunday	Monday	Tuesday	Wednesday	Thursday	Friday	Saturday
	Having a positive mental attitude is asking how something can be done rather than saying it can't be done. (Bo Bennett)			**1** ✉ f t Send March email newsletter and offers	**2** f t **March is Employee Spirit Month**	**3** **Unique Names Day**
4	**5**	**6** f t	**7**	**8** **Working Womens Day**	**9** 🔶 f t	**10**
11 Daylight Saving Time Begins	**12**	**13** f t Look ahead! Finalize April details and plan May and June	**14**	**15** **Consumer Rights Day**	**16** f t **Lips Appreciation Day**	**17** St. Patricks Day
18	**19**	**20** ✉ f t Send email: March 'Last Chance!' and April/May preview	**21** **First Day of Spring**	**22**	**23** 🔶 f t	**24**
25	**26**	**27** f t Begin promoting for Mother's Day (Sunday, May 13)	**28**	**29** f t	**30**	**31** Take/break down expired promotions; set up for April

score card

Check one box for every communication task completed from the above calendar this month:

week one
☐ ☐ ☐ ☐ ☐

week two
☐ ☐ ☐ ☐ ☐

week three
☐ ☐ ☐ ☐

week four
☐ ☐ ☐ ☐ ☐

week five
☐ ☐ ☐ ☐

_____# of **New Clients**
Up/Down from last month #_____

_____# of **Retail Products** sold
Up/Down from last month #_____

f _____# of Facebook Fans/Friends
Up/Down from last month #_____

t _____# of Twitter Followers
Up/Down from last month #_____

🔶 _____# of Blog Hits/Readers
Up/Down from last month #_____

✉ _____# of Email Subscribers
Up/Down from last month #_____

_____# of Email Opens (if known)
Up/Down from last month #_____

plan ahead

One class, seminar or webinar you'll attend in the next 2 months:

_____

One technique or technical skill you will improve or master next month:

_____

One thing you resolve to change in your work or personal life next month:

_____

_____

Intrigue, Engage, Provoke

The editors of television reality shows condense what they feel are the most compelling, provocative, exciting and important conversations, activities and events that occur over the course of a week or even longer, into a one or two hour-long show.

That might mean they reduce one hundred and sixty eight hours (more than ten thousand minutes) into just 35 or 40 minutes of actual show time when you account for commercials and "coming up next" teasers.

They try to produce the most intriguing, engaging and provocative episode possible in order to entice viewers to watch the show, to follow contestants, to visit their web sites and, in some cases, even to decide the outcome of the series via public vote.

What does this have to do with styling?

Think about each client visit as a condensed, exaggerated reality show. Your client only gets to see, hear, smell and experience the elements that you decide to edit down into the 30 or 60 minutes of time they are at their appointment.

Realizing that **you are** the producer and real time editor of the **client's 'show,'** how can you make sure each one is **intriguing, engaging** and **provocative to the client?** And what does that mean?

- **Intrigue: (verb) meaning to fascinate, arouse the curiosity of, or amuse.**

To be intriguing is to be at the same time both enticing and mysterious. If you are intrigued by a business, you only know some things about it, but not everything, and what you do know makes you want to know more. You are willing to be drawn deeper into experience with them.

Intrigue also implies mystery. If your clients are intrigued by you as a stylist, they consciously or subconsciously feel that they do not already know all that you can do for them, but they do know that you have more to offer. They want to find out what else you can do for them.

And if you think creating intrigue sounds nice, just wait until you know what stimulating full-on client-engagement can do for you!

When your client experience is powerfully-positive enough to actually engage a client, you can expect them not only to read your communications and try new products and services; they will do even more.

- **Engaged clients view themselves as insiders, part of your 'club' if you will.**

They will attend and enjoy your events and bring people with them. They will participate in two-way dialogue with you, provide you with constructive feedback, and even help you generate new ideas. They will respond to your questions on Facebook and leave reviews for you. The engaged customer will vote for you in online "best of" polls. They will be an active source of referrals and they will work to earn rewards and participate in your programs.

Engaged clients believe they are part of something. They believe they are important to you and to your business. Apart from having a family or social connection to your business, the only way a client will become engaged will be because you deliberately plan and provide consistent client experiences that demonstrate to them, over the passage of time, clearly and unmistakably, that they are a **unique, valued** and **vitally important person** in your life, personally, as well as your business.

- **It's not that they love you, it's that you have shown them they are important *to you*.**

Think about it in romantic terms. Would you 'engage' or commit yourself to a long-term relationship with someone if you didn't believe they truly cared about you—enough so that they care about you more than themselves and put your interests above theirs?

That's what it takes to stimulate engagement!

Intrigue motivates clients to find out more or even to try more and engaged clients will be interacting with your salon or spa in even more meaningful ways. **But at its most powerful, the client experience is also provocative.**

Being provocative to your clients is next-level. An involvement of the emotions and the senses, this word often embodies the idea of desire that is a reflection of both love and lust, both need and want.

- **Provocative is a word that implies both accompanying action and intent.**

When used in a romantic connotation, the word 'provocative' implies that one party is purposefully and intentionally acting in order to stimulate an emotional response in another that will be demonstrated by acts of passion, affection and love.

To provoke someone means that you are intelligently, intentionally doing certain things that are specifically designed to stimulate desired responses and actions on the part of someone else.

- **To be provocative is a powerful thing!**

If you are not intelligently and intentionally designing each customer experience from beginning-to-end, then you are leaving some of the details up to chance.

You are missing opportunities to stimulate engagement and loyalty.

And some of the details that you are missing or leaving to chance may actually be working against the experience that you want to create. This may be why some of the customer reactions and responses that you are provoking are not what you expected or desired.

The client experience lasts a couple of hours at most. It is a compressed, exaggerated, condensed version of all of the points of contact that any one person has with your business. They don't see all that goes on behind the scenes.

You only have a very small amount of time with any one individual to win their repeat business, loyalty and referrals. The question is, how will you, as the editor and producer of their reality show, work to edit each 'episode' down to its most intriguing, engaging and provocative best in order to keep each client watching?

March
Extras

Being Provocative

It can be difficult to get people to comment, 'like' and share social media posts for the simple reason that people are bombarded with so many of them every day. One way to do this is by using questions, polls and provocative statements and topics. When you touch on something people are passionate about, you'll get their attention.

Here are some topics that provoke engagement in social media:

- **Coffee**
  For whatever reason, post a quote about coffee or tell people that you're enjoying a venti non-fat, no-whip pumpkin spice latte and you'll get 'likes,' comments and envy.

  You can also post stats about caffeine, recipes for holiday, dessert or drink coffees or even pictures showing off the perfect java concoction.

- **The battle of the sexes**
  Stats or comments about women vs. male drivers, shoppers, grooming habits— there are so many stereotypical differences you can touch on!

- **Inspiring quotes**
  Everyone has rough patches in life. Everyone has bad days. Everyone deals with difficult people. Using quotes that speak to these as well as encourage us to keep going, tough it out, be the better person— these type of quotes resound with everyone.

TIP: To keep the 'share' connected with your business, put your business signature on the quote or image after giving credit to the original quote source.

Use holidays, observances and themes as the basis to connect, engage and educate your prospects (aka "future clients") and current customers.

April is Customer Loyalty and Customer Appreciation Month

The secret for business success is not just attracting new clients or getting one sale, it's engaging your clients over the long haul.

Engaged clients believe they are part of something. They believe they are important to you **and** to your business.

Apart from having a family or social connection to you, the only way a client will become engaged will be because you deliberately plan and provide consistent client experiences that demonstrate to them, over the passage of time, clearly and unmistakably, that they are a **unique**, **valued** and **vitally important** person in your life, **personally,** as well as your business.

It's not that they love you or even the products or services your business provides.

It's that you've convinced them that they are important to you.

Think about it in romantic terms.

Would you 'engage' or commit yourself to a long-term relationship with someone if you didn't believe that they truly cared about you—enough so that they care about you more than themselves and put your interests above theirs?

Communication is Key

Many salons contact clients who have lapsed after 3-6 months—it's too long. If you haven't seen someone in 3-6 months, you've likely lost them! This is where social media and email marketing can help keep you connected.

Make staying in touch with your clients on a regular basis a top priority!

April 1-7 - Laugh at Work Week

- Post April Fools Day or random quotes, weird facts, dumb jokes, links to short comedy videos and off-the-wall observations on Facebook, Twitter, your blog, customer email newsletter and employee newsletter or bulletin board.

- Make humorous or April Fools type 'public announcements' during the day to give customers a chuckle or write a humorous version of your newsletter.

- Hold a best funny story, prank or joke contest on Facebook and Twitter.

April 11 - Siblings Day

Solicit heartwarming (or hilarious) sibling stories online and in-salon. Turn your blog, Facebook page and email newsletter into a forum for people to post loving and appreciative sentiments to their siblings.

April 16 - Income Tax Pay Day

Go to your local post office on the evening of April 16th (because the 15th falls on a Sunday in 2012) and give out business cards, bounce-back offers, samples, refreshments and/or branded tchotchkes to those waiting in line to mail their tax returns at the last minute. Repeat this exercise for other community events, city parades, people waiting in lines in front of clubs or stores, etc.

April 20 - Wear Your Pajamas Day

- Wear your pajamas today—why not? As a public relations stunt, work in pajamas to raise awareness and solicit donations for a local charity or needy family.

- Hold a "wear your pajamas day" happy hour or open house or invite clients to shop in their pajamas all day long or at a specific event.

April 26 - Tell a Story Day

Do your clients know why you became a stylist? Do they know why you are passionately concerned for their best interests? Have you given them reasons to relate to you as a person—not just a professional?

When your customers feel that you truly have their best interests at heart and they feel *personally* connected to you, they will be that much more likely to purchase retail products and additional services on your recommendation and to refer friends and family to you. Tell your story on your Blog and Facebook page and in your email newsletter.

 Facebook    Twitter   Blog    Email/Mail

April

Sunday	Monday	Tuesday	Wednesday	Thursday	Friday	Saturday
1 **Customer Loyalty and Appreciation Month** **April Fools Day**	**2** **Laugh at Work Week April 1-7**	✉ f t **3** Send April email newsletter and offers	**4**	**5** f t	**6**	**7**
8 **Easter**	**9**	f t **10**	**11**	**12**	📶 f t **13**	**14**
15	**16** **Income Tax Pay Day**	f t **17** Look ahead! Finalize May details and plan June and July	**18**	**19** f t	**20** **Wear Your Pajamas Day**	**21**
22	**23** Begin promoting bridal, graduation and summer seasonal offers	✉ f t **24** Send email: April 'Last Chance!' and May/June preview	**25**	**26** **Tell a Story Day**	📶 f t **27**	**28**
29	**30** Take/break down expired promotions; set up for May				If we don't take care of our customers, someone else will. (Anonymous)	

score card

Check one box for every communication task completed from the above calendar this month:

week one
☐ ☐ ☐ ☐ ☐

week two
☐ ☐ ☐ ☐ ☐

week three
☐ ☐ ☐ ☐

week four
☐ ☐ ☐ ☐ ☐ ☐

_____ # of **New Clients**
Up/Down from last month #_____

_____ # of **Retail Products** sold
Up/Down from last month #_____

 _____ # of Facebook Fans/Friends
Up/Down from last month #_____

 _____ # of Twitter Followers
Up/Down from last month #_____

📶 _____ # of Blog Hits/Readers
Up/Down from last month #_____

✉ _____ # of Email Subscribers
Up/Down from last month #_____

_____ # of Email Opens (if known)
Up/Down from last month #_____

plan ahead

One class, seminar or webinar you'll attend in the next 2 months:

_____

One technique or technical skill you will improve or master next month:

_____

One thing you resolve to change in your work or personal life next month:

_____

The Client Touch Point

Nothing is healthier for your business or will do more to alleviate your personal stress (April is Stress Awareness Month!) than cultivating a happy, loyal client base.

Retention and loyalty initiatives may require the investment of time, supplies or money on your part; but did you know—it can cost **5 times** as much (or even more) to gain new clients than it does to retain current clients.

The steps you take to ensure your clients will return, and that they will do so at the frequency you desire, are worth the effort!

One of the keys to customer retention is good old "customer satisfaction," and this requires that you actively solicit, obtain and honestly analyze customer feedback—good or bad.

Analyze the client experience from their first visit to your website, receipt of an advertisement, or the placing of that first phone call to your business through to the points that would comprise the end of their experience or visit.

Evaluate each aspect of a customer's journey at every possible touch point, because you never know where you might be losing customer interest or may be failing to live up to their expectations in some way.

You could be losing prospective and current customers at <u>any</u> of the following touch points:

- Ads designed to draw in a new customer

- Offers or new client reward designed to draw in a new customer

- Website landing page, targeted offer pages, site navigation, "contact" or "directions"

- Facebook page, blog and other social media sites

- Responses to "new customer" inquiries via telephone, email, website or social media sites

- Incoming call answering, automated messages or on-hold messages

- After hours outgoing telephone messages

- Performance of referral rewards system

- Ease of finding your location and parking

- Outside of store (or outside of business park) or web store landing page

- Window displays and signage on doors, windows or anything on the outside meant to draw the customer in (or lack of anything to help draw a customer in)

- If and how the customer is greeted when they arrive

- If and how/where the customer is directed to begin shopping or get directions

- Where and how the customer checks in for an appointment or scheduled visit

- Waiting area or length of wait

- Furnishings or decor

- Refreshments or hospitality stations (free or for pay)

- Rest rooms

- Ease of shopping, ease of finding desired items in store or online

- Friendliness of support staff such as receptionist, bookkeeper, assistants or aides

- Professionalism of any professional care or service providers and support staff, perception of knowledge, education and expertise

- Prescriptive advice for professional or home-use products, or the "you might also like" suggested selling on web store

- Knowledge of staff about products or services, online descriptions of products or services (even if purchases will be made in-store)

- Staff ability to up-sell, knowledge of products, ability to suggest upgrades and add-ons

- Any point where the customer or prospect is asked for contact information or asked to subscribe to communications

- Ease of point of purchase or check out experience

- Length or complexity of check out, staff ability and attitude, self check out options, etc.

- Helpfulness and availability of staff at the point of check out

- If and how the customer is thanked before leaving

- How the customer is dismissed or told 'goodbye'

- What happens after the visit; follow-up, bounce-back offer, re-booking process, surveys, etc.

- Experience at home with products purchased or results of services

That's more than **30 touch points** which can **damage or enhance** a **customer's experience** with your business!

It is the attention you devote to making the customer experience truly special—the 'extra' things you do—that tells the client you are personally interested in their well-being, louder than any words you speak.

And it is the extent to which you intelligently and intentionally create an ideal client experience that will **set you apart from the competition**, making you **the one to watch,** ensuring that clients feel you truly value their business (rather than take it for granted).

A Simple Personal Act
(that cultivates loyalty)

People will notice if you take the time to do something personal for them. A personal thank-you note written to each service client or at least to your most important or influential customers (those who do a significant amount of business with you or those likely to refer and influence others) would take only **minutes** a day. You can even pre-address and begin each note prior to your encounter with each client.

It costs little (email costs even less), but will go a long way toward strengthening your relationships with clients and keeping your services in the forefront of your clients minds.

A hand-written note is a personal touch in an impersonal world. It conveys your gratitude for their patronage—for them choosing your business—when there are so many others they could choose.

Giving a personal thank-you note or sending an email gives you the opportunity to connect with your customer by remarking on a topic of conversation or an area of concern they shared with you (showing that you really listened and truly care about what is important to them).

It's an opportunity to ask them to book another appointment, to return soon or consider you for other services.

It's an opportunity to mention new products or services, mention those you spoke about during their last visit or make gift suggestions.

It's an opportunity to ask for referrals. It's an opportunity to ask questions meant to get feedback that can help you improve the client experience, such as:

- Whether they were satisfied with a specific service or product or their overall experience

- Whether they have any questions about the products or services they purchased

- If there was any way in which their experience could have been improved

- Whether they were able to find all they wanted—do you carry what they were looking for and/or was it in stock

Writing a personal note is a **very simple act** that can be completed in a few minutes; but still, **few people** are doing it. If you make this part of **your routine**, it will get noticed, **it will set you apart, making you the one to watch.** It will bring clients back and it will stimulate more referrals. It will provide you with more opportunities to truly connect with your clients.

Use holidays, observances and themes as the basis to connect, engage and educate your prospects (aka "future clients") and current customers.

Get the Picture?
(May is National Photograph Month)

There are a lot of ways you can partner with local photographers, and lots of great reasons for you to do so! They can work with you on photo shoots for use in advertising, attend and photo-document customer and corporate events, photograph your work for use in marketing and press releases, provide you with photographs to help you create your own catalog, recipe books, coffee table books or marketing calendars, help you make employee I.D. badges or child I.D. cards and more. You can be a source of cross-referrals for them, giving them marketing access to your customers and referring people to them for weddings, graduation, family and holiday pictures and other photo-worthy events.

Here are some ways you can market cooperatively or create joint offers with a photographer:

- Major life events, family photos, Christmas and Holiday card photos, anniversaries, family reunions, engagements, weddings and receptions

- Events: holiday parties, corporate events, conventions, graduation, prom, etc.

- School photos, senior photos, school events, competitions, fine arts performances, prom, homecoming, graduation

- Head shots, photo shoots, social media profile photos, corporate blog and website photos, professional corporate publication photos

- Before-and-After photos for makeovers or to document major life external transformation projects (such as restorative or cosmetic surgeries, weight loss programs, etc.) or before-and-after shots for events or contests (like for celebrity look alike makeovers)

- Holiday events, sales and offers

- Catalog, brochure or other marketing collateral featuring your staff, products, services, building, customers, etc.

- Public relations stunts, charity benefit events and fundraisers, corporate meetings, employee-appreciation events, etc.

May 5 - Cinco de Mayo

- In honor of Cinco de Mayo, extend a $5 promotion to clients such as $5 off every $50 spent in May on retail and/or services or $5 off a specific service or product.

- Post interesting facts or have a trivia contest about Cinco de Mayo and related traditions on your Facebook page, at an event or in-salon.

May 10 - Tourist Appreciation Day

- Hold an open house event where you treat guests like 'tourists.' Give tours. Collect contact information. Create a punch card designed to look like a ticket or map and have guests "check in" at each stop in order to learn more about products and services, receive samples, consultations and demonstrations.

- Reward participants when they have visited all the stops on your "tour." Hold one or more door prize drawings at the event and collect contact information to add to your database. Send attendees home with information about products or services featured at the event and a bounce-back offer. Follow up by email.

- Send information about your services to individuals who cater to tourists such as the employees of hotels and motels. Let them know that you can provide fast, traveler-friendly makeover and touch up services for their out-of-town guests.

May 13-19 - Work At Home Moms Week

- Extend a special offer to work-at-home moms.

- Take nominations for exceptional work-at-home moms, or hold a drawing to reward one or more local work-at-home moms with a pampering or makeover service, product or prize package.

- Create Work-at-Home Mom Makeover packages that will help them stay in style no matter where they work.

- Reach out to stay-at-home mom niche groups, like MOPS (Mother's of PreSchoolers) with an invitation or special offer to try your services.

- Do you have slow daytime hours during the week? Attract work-at-home moms by offering free add-ons or offering special rates on products or services sold during slower hours, or hold a work-at-home moms networking or social event.

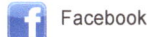 Facebook    Twitter   Blog    Email/Mail

May

Sunday	Monday	Tuesday	Wednesday	Thursday	Friday	Saturday
		1 ✉ f t Send May email newsletter and offers	2 **May is National Photography Month**	3 f t	4	5 **Cinco de Mayo**
6	7	8 f t Begin promoting for Father's Day (Sunday, June 17)	9	10 **Tourist Appreciation Day**	11 🔶 f t	12
13 f t **Mothers Day** Send Mothers Day Greeting	14 **Work at Home Moms Week May 13-19**	15 f t Look ahead! Finalize June details and plan July and August	16	17	18 f t	19
20	21	22 ✉ f t Send email: May 'Last Chance!' and June/July preview	23	24 🔶 f t	25	26
27	28 f t **Memorial Day** Post Memorial Day Quote or Sentiment	29	30	31 Take/break down expired promotions; set up for June	*Courage is like a muscle; we strengthen it with use.* (Ruth Gordon)	

score card

Check one box for every communication task completed from the above calendar this month:

week one
☐ ☐ ☐ ☐ ☐

week two
☐ ☐ ☐ ☐

week three
☐ ☐ ☐ ☐ ☐ ☐

week four
☐ ☐ ☐ ☐ ☐

week five
☐ ☐

_____ # of **New Clients**
Up/Down from last month #_____

_____ # of **Retail Products** sold
Up/Down from last month #_____

f _____ # of Facebook Fans/Friends
Up/Down from last month #_____

t _____ # of Twitter Followers
Up/Down from last month #_____

🔶 _____ # of Blog Hits/Readers
Up/Down from last month #_____

✉ _____ # of Email Subscribers
Up/Down from last month #_____

_____ # of Email Opens (if known)
Up/Down from last month #_____

plan ahead

One class, seminar or webinar you'll attend in the next 2 months:

_____

One technique or technical skill you will improve or master next month:

_____

One thing you resolve to change in your work or personal life next month:

_____

_____

Change the Way You Play the Game to Sell More Retail

To **sell more retail** you have to **build client trust**. To **build client trust,** you have to **sell more retail!**

Here's why:

- Selling the right products to your clients is **your responsibility;** you are likely the **only** person who will observe their hair, scalp or skin conditions and know how to improve or treat them.

- Selling clients the right products gives them the tools they **need** to meet long-term goals for looks they want to achieve, the quality of their appearance and their hair-scalp-nail-skin health.

- Selling products keeps you on the client's mind; when they use your products at home they will remember the advice and instructions you gave and will watch for the benefits you predicted to materialize.

- Smell is one of the most powerful memory triggers. Selling professional products (which are designed with painstaking attention to fragrance as well as performance) will stimulate subconscious memories of how clients felt relaxed, pampered, special and important while in your care at the salon or spa.

- Products that perform as advertised and deliver on benefits give clients a reason to come to back to your salon or spa in order to repurchase.

- Selling products which perform as you said they would reinforces the client's confidence in **your knowledge, expertise and ability**. Product prescription and performance proves that **you** are the expert!

Now that you know why, here's how:

- First and foremost: always and only make authentic recommendations. If you sell for your own benefit (rather than a client's genuine need) you will lose trust. Once lost, trust is difficult to regain.

- Use a visual take-away tool, like a prescription form, business card with an area to list recommendations or some other system, religiously, as part of each and every client appointment. There are free prescription form templates available on the resources page of my website at www.12monthsofmarketing.net.

- Change your mindset. You are a service provider, and making product recommendations is part of that service. You have a professional obligation to tell clients about what you observe and how products and services can help.

- Talk about problems and solutions, not products. Talk about conditions and cures. Talk about the client's goals—like achieving a celebrity look—in terms of products needed for styling and maintenance at home, makeup palette and step-by-step procedures, highlights, hair color or texture, etc.

- Talk in terms of benefits to the client, not the virtue or 'newness' of any product. It's not that you have a great new product that does such-and-such, it's that your client needs a product because it provides certain specific, unique client benefits. See the difference?

- Put selling tools to work on your behalf. Merchandise, (focusing on client-centric benefits) from the inside-out. Website and blog posts, email newsletters, postcards, social media status updates, posters on windows and walls, shelf and station talkers, point of sale displays, samples, 'try me' stations, bag stuffers, thank you notes or emails, prescription pads, recommendation cards and appointment reminders—at least 15 ways to introduce your clients to the products they need—without saying a word!

- Reformulate pricing to include products in the price of certain services, (such as texture or hair color services) where you know that reparative, reconstructing or color extending products are needed. That way, you're a hero—you're "giving" products to your clients! Or bundle products into combination packages.

Taffy and Sticky Marketing

National Taffy Day is in May.

When I think about taffy from the standpoint of analogy, two principles come to mind; **the first is flexibility.**

When taffy is fresh, it's malleable, flexible; you can work with it, you can stretch and reshape it without breaking it. What a great principle for you as a leader as well as for your business.

When it comes to dealing with other people, are you flexible? Are you able to stretch yourself to new lengths?

The next time you field a customer complaint, a challenging employee or an unusual situation in your business, "be the taffy."

Be willing to be stretched and folded over and over again, blended with new experiences and reshaped into the best piece of taffy you can be!

The second principle that struck me had to do with stickiness.

When people talk about 'sticky marketing' they are talking about how memorable your efforts are with your audience. Do your clients connect with and remember your marketing messages?

If you practice one-and-done marketing, your messages aren't likely to be very sticky in the minds of customers.

Creating a strong brand across all marketing channels (and across all customer and employee touch points) requires the delivery of multiple messages, delivered consistently and clearly, over time and across all of your customer touch points in order to penetrate the minds of consumers.

There aren't shortcuts; this is the only way to **build marketing** that **sticks in the minds** of customers.

The same holds true for single marketing campaigns. You can't just tell customers about a product or service one time and expect that they will jump for joy and elation and rush to book an appointment.

It might take months and a dozen messages before customers suddenly "remember" that new product or service you have that they all-of-a-sudden can't live without.

Consistency and constancy are the keys to sticky marketing!

BONUS: Here's how to put Taffy Day to work to build your business:

- Fill a large container with taffy pieces (count first!) and hold a quantity-guessing contest. Take entries in-salon and online allowing people to enter via print or web form, Facebook post, email reply, etc. Use entries as a means of collecting contact information to grow your database or get more email subscribers, Facebook and other social media followers. After the contest, extend a special offer to all entrants.

- Purchase branded taffy or partner with a local candy or gourmet foods store to provide samples of taffy to gift-with-purchase, sell or use as contest prizes. Give gourmet taffy to your most valuable customers.

- Post facts about taffy or taffy making on your Facebook page, blog and email newsletter. Hold a taffy trivia contest. Solicit taffy recipes or have a taffy making contest, tasting or happy hour.

Use holidays, observances and themes as the basis to connect, engage and educate your prospects (aka "future clients") and current customers.

June is Effective Communication Month

Long gone are the days when a marketing strategy included just an occasional postcard, flyer or Yellow Pages listing. It's never been easier to get marketing messages out into the public sphere; but for the same reason, it's never been harder to get noticed. You can't afford to believe you don't need an electronic marketing toolbox—one stuffed to the gills with hard-working tools in prime condition that you'll take out and put to work nearly every day.

Here are the basics, plus an overview of the four most popular forms of social media marketing, so that you'll know where to start:

- A website or online portfolio with your own domain name. Research shows that buyers go to corporate sites before making purchase decisions, even if drawn by social media, so social media and blogs aren't web site substitutes. You need to own your own electronic space, even if it's no more than a few simple but well-designed, engaging pages.

- Email marketing. Social media isn't a substitute; email is more intimate and more engaging. Email marketing is powerful; it gives your business a voice, the means to put valuable information and compelling offers right in front of your clients at home.

Social Media Primer: In 2011, a Social Media Examiner (www.socialmediaexaminer.com) report noted the **4 most popular, effective social media sites** for business:

1. Facebook. Why? **1 out of every 8 minutes spent online** is spent on Facebook (Hubspot.com). Use Facebook to engage people who like you, share expert information, make announcements, solicit feedback and use the personality of your business to attract prospects. Use giveaways and contests to spark engagement, help fill the books during slow hours and stimulate event RSVPs.

2. Twitter messages are like 140 character social media posts with A.D.D. Using Twitter for business won't take a lot of time and helps to share your website, blog, email marketing and social media posts farther and wider.

3. LinkedIn, for networking with peers and industry professionals. It won't take up too much time and you can cross post from your website, email, blog and Facebook.

4. Blogging is a great way to build your reputation as an expert. Just like social media, it's not the place to push in hard-sell style; instead, educate, build awareness and enhance your expert reputation. Use Top 10 lists and "Did you know..." posts to talk about new products, services, celebrity looks and fashion, etc.

June 1 – Flip a Coin Day

- Provide some excitement for customers by letting them flip a coin when they arrive or at the cash register for a chance to receive free or specially priced add-ons, samples, branded items, extra rewards or points.

- If you're feeling really brave, hold a drawing for one customer to win a chance to flip a coin to determine whether you or they will pay their bill.

June 10-16 – Business Etiquette Week

- Send a note of thanks, a token of appreciation or extend an appreciative offer to the owners and/or employees of businesses located near yours or to vendors, landlord, marketing partners, etc.

- Review your own collateral and business cards. Is it time for an update? Is any information obsolete or incorrect? Does your logo look like something from another decade? Update and/or redesign your collateral in such a way that it communicates something authentic about you and your business, and captures the attention and interest of the reader.

June 26 – Coin a Phrase Day

- Hold a contest to see who can come up with the best new phrase about one of your services or products.

- Include a coined phrase in email or other marketing collateral and reward customers who return to your business and use the phrase at the point of purchase.

- Hold a trivia contest or post entries about the origin of common-but-wacky phrases used in society currently or in the past on your Facebook page, blog, email newsletter and bag stuffers.

 Facebook   Twitter   Blog    Email/Mail

June

Sunday	Monday	Tuesday	Wednesday	Thursday	Friday	Saturday
		Two monologues don't make a dialogue. (Jeff Daly)		**June is Effective Communications Month**	✉ f t 1 **Flip a Coin Day** Send June email newsletter and offers	2
3	4	f t 5	6	7	🔶 f t 8	9
10	11 **Business Etiquette Week June 10-16**	f t 12 Look ahead! Finalize July details and plan Aug. and Sept.	13	14	f t 15	16
f t 17 **Fathers Day** Send Fathers Day Greeting	18	✉ f t 19 Send email: June 'Last Chance!' and July/Aug preview	20	21	🔶 f t 22	23
24	25	f t 26 **Coin a Phrase Day**	27	28	f t 29	30 Take/break down expired promotions; set up for July

score card

Check one box for every communication task completed from the above calendar this month:

week one
☐ ☐ ☐

week two
☐ ☐ ☐ ☐ ☐

week three
☐ ☐ ☐ ☐

week four
☐ ☐ ☐ ☐ ☐
☐ ☐

week five
☐ ☐ ☐ ☐

_____ # of **New Clients**
Up/Down from last month #_____

_____ # of **Retail Products** sold
Up/Down from last month #_____

f _____ # of Facebook Fans/Friends
Up/Down from last month #_____

t _____ # of Twitter Followers
Up/Down from last month #_____

🔶 _____ # of Blog Hits/Readers
Up/Down from last month #_____

✉ _____ # of Email Subscribers
Up/Down from last month #_____

_____ # of Email Opens (if known)
Up/Down from last month #_____

plan ahead

One class, seminar or webinar you'll attend in the next 2 months:
_____

One technique or technical skill you will improve or master next month:
_____

One thing you resolve to change in your work or personal life next month:
_____
_____

Marketing Lingo

Marketing, advertising, public relations, branding, word-of-mouth, buzz, viral or cause marketing— all terms often used without a true understanding of what they mean. But their real power lies in their true meanings and the words used to describe them:

Everything about your business is marketing. Why?

"Marketing" includes **all** the activities, means and tactics undertaken to **identify, attract, satisfy, engage, motivate (to take desired actions) and retain customers.** From traditional ads, flyers and door hangers to social media, events, your employee culture, policies, products, services, décor – *everything* about your business is sending a marketing message.

The question is, what messages are they sending?

Here are some common marketing terms you should familiarize yourself with:

Advertising:
drawing attention to a business, event, product, service, etc., in a public medium in order to get people to take specific actions (visit, attend, buy, etc.)

Public Relations:
tactics used to develop and maintain a favorable public image for a business or an individual.

Branding:
often thought of as applying one's logo, typeface, colors and other visual and audio symbols to corporate communications, décor, etc.; but branding is much more. Your brand isn't something you can see—it's really the perceptions that exist in the minds of people, built each and every time they interact with you or any aspect of your business. Run into a customer at the grocery store? Your brand just got built up (or taken down) a little bit more. To really brand your business, you must analyze and intentionally design all of the variables that might occur at every touch point to build the best possible experience for customers and prospects.

Word of Mouth Marketing:
the passing of information about your business from person to person. Often confused with doing nothing yet hoping people will accidentally talk about you or your business— remember, people won't talk about your business unless and until you give them something to talk about!

Buzz Marketing:
a word-of-mouth marketing technique wherein a business tries to make interactions with customers appear to be unique, spontaneous exchanges of information, rather than delivery of pre-scripted marketing pitches.

Viral Marketing:
"...is an idea that spreads... and while spreading actually helps market your business or cause." (Seth Godin, sethgodin.typepad.com)

Cause Marketing:
cooperative efforts of a for-profit business and a non-profit organization for mutual benefit.

Cooperative Marketing:
marketing activities you do in cooperation with other salon or spa professionals or with other businesses in pursuit of shared goals.

Cross Marketing
marketing activities you agree to do with another professional or business whereby they will recommend or allow you promote your services to their clients, and you will present their products or services to yours.

One additional benefit of both Cooperative and Cross-Marketing is the implied endorsement of the businesses you partner with.

Since you are—*essentially*—recommending that your clients do business with your marketing partners, expose your clients only to those businesses that will treat them as good as you do!

Marketing Tools

It isn't enough to ensure client-centric experiences in the chair; you have to view every client touch point through the eyes of clients and prospects, including your communications. While some salons and spas have multiple channels of communication open to and from customers, some have yet to build channels out beyond use of the telephone and in-salon signage.

Some of the **basic tools** that are (or could be) at your disposal:

- Business Cards (general)
- Business Cards (with client referral or rewards form)
- Business Cards (with seasonal or new client offer)
- "Ask Me About" titled product or event display/station talker cards, celebrity-endorsement "As Seen In" display sheets and shelf talkers
- Reminders (via phone, text, email or direct mail per client's preference!) Appointment reminders have been shown to significantly reduce no-shows and rescheduling.
- Doctor and other offices use "intake forms" all the time. Create your own client "intake" or update form (or ask the client to re-verify their information verbally at each appointment) and include a question asking for their preference when it comes to appointment reminders.
- Note Cards (blank)
- Note Cards (thank you, sympathy, congratulations and birthday)
- Postcards (direct mail or use as bag stuffers, handbills, station talkers)
- Postcards (sent in stacks to be placed in the break rooms of local large employers, your business park, schools, etc.)
- Signage (both for inside and outside of the salon or spa)
- Merchandising

- Flyers (direct mail, post as PDF online, bag stuffers, business-to-business offers, event handouts)
- Press Release template
- Invitations
- RSVP return mail and/or online forms
- Menus (general)
- Menus (special menus for events, special occasions, or specific service groups such as bridal or corporate events)
- Menus (pre-sold series purchase opportunities)
- Menus (combination menus featuring your offers as well as those of your business cross and cooperative marketing partners)
- Web site
- Email (personal)
- Email (marketing, such as Constant Contact—you don't want to send bulk marketing messages from your personal email account for many reasons)
- Facebook (and/or other social sites, most if not all are free to use)
- Blog (free to set up and use on sites like blogger.com)
- Rewards, Loyalty and Referral Program support materials

Use holidays, observances and themes as the basis to connect, engage and educate your prospects (aka "future clients") and current customers.

6 Ways to Keep Color Clients
in the Salon:

Because of the slow economy many clients who used to receive color services in the salon now extend the time in between regular appointments by weeks or even do their own color at home. Here are 6 ways to keep color clients in the salon, under your care!

1. Educate your clients. If they believe in-salon hair color, administered by a professional colorist is equivalent to buying drugstore color to use at home, you're failing to educate your clients that:

   • Your products are superior because (insert the ways your products benefit the client, here).

   • You choose different products, toners, colors, etc., based not only on desired color outcome but also your client's current color, hair condition and type and even environmental conditions—what boxed drugstore color can do that?

   • Your services include conditioning services needed to restore and protect the hair from chemical damage, and result in less damage to the hair.

   • Show before-and-after pictures showing the pitfalls of at-home color experiments and/or the amazing color results you produce in the salon.

2. Be more creative. Rather than applying all-over color every 6 weeks, can the time between applications be extended slightly and/or could you develop an "in-between" touch up for the hair color at the 6 week mark that would be less expensive?

3. Do the work of budgeting for your clients. Add up the cost of all the services a client would receive over the course of the year and break it down in to flat rate monthly payments. This also gives you the chance to pre-book a client out for an entire year!   For customers that pre-book and pre-pay, offer a VIP customer discount, or include a free retail product as a gift with each service.

4. Party on! Create group appointment blocks for color clients (or even hold "color party" events for groups of friends). These blocks of time allow you to maximize the use of your time, serving more than one color client at a time in a color 'party.' Party rates would allow you to lower the cost for everyone, since you would be serving multiple clients at the same time.

5. Give away "free" retail. Build the cost of an average retail product (such as a color-enhancing or extending shampoo or conditioner) into the cost of your color services.

6. Take your show on the road. Friends gather in groups to enjoy jeans parties, jewelry parties, lingerie parties, etc. Chances are you even have independent party-type sellers among your clients. Partner with one or more of these and attend their parties. Show off by giving a blowout or hairstyling demo and free consultations for all attendees. Distribute written prescriptions or service recommendations and set up appointments for those interested. Provide an incentive for those who book an appointment on the spot. (A free sample prescription form is available on the resources page at www.12monthsofmarketing.net).

July 4 – Independence Day

Participate in summer community events (including those for Independence Day). If your city has a parade, hand out business cards, flyers and samples. Hand out ice-cold branded bottled waters. Distribute branded calendars, rulers, pens, lip balms or other items people are likely to keep and use.

July 12 – Compliment Your Mirror Day

• Hold a contest to see who can come up with the best "Mirror, mirror, on the wall…" phrase ending.

• Help clients get the answers they want from their mirrors. Create special offers around the products needed to recreate celebrity looks or current trends at home.

July 19 – Lollipop Day

• Place lollipops in a large glass container and hold a contest to see who can guess how many are inside. Post a picture of the container on your blog, email newsletter and Facebook page so people can enter online as well as in-salon. Add contact information from entry forms to your database. After the contest, send an email to announce the name of the winner and extend a bounce-back offer to all entrants.

• Post trivia or history about lollipops on your Facebook page or hold a trivia contest.

• Gift lollipops to schools, local day cares or churches along with your business card and a new client offer for parents and staff. Or send a lollipop bouquet along with your cards and offer to the receptionists of local businesses for lunch or break room placement.

Facebook Twitter Blog  Email/Mail

July

Sunday	Monday	Tuesday	Wednesday	Thursday	Friday	Saturday
1	2	✉ f t 3 Send July email newsletter and offers	4 **Independence Day**	5	f t 6	7
8	9	f t 10	11	12 **Compliment Your Mirror Day**	📶 f t 13	14
15	16	f t 17 Look ahead! Finalize August details and plan Sept. and Oct.	18	19 **Lollipop Day**	f t 20	21
22	23 Begin promoting for back to school	✉ f t 24 Send email: July 'Last Chance!' and Aug/Sept preview	25	26	📶 f t 27	28
29	30	f t 31 Take/break down expired promotions; set up for August		You can't run in place or someone will pass you by. (Jim Valvano)		

score card

Check one box for every communication task completed from the above calendar this month:

week one
☐ ☐ ☐ ☐ ☐

week two
☐ ☐ ☐ ☐ ☐

week three
☐ ☐ ☐ ☐

week four
☐ ☐ ☐ ☐ ☐ ☐

week five
☐ ☐

_____ # of **New Clients**
Up/Down from last month #_____

_____ # of **Retail Products** sold
Up/Down from last month #_____

 _____ # of Facebook Fans/Friends
Up/Down from last month #_____

 _____ # of Twitter Followers
Up/Down from last month #_____

📶 _____ # of Blog Hits/Readers
Up/Down from last month #_____

✉ _____ # of Email Subscribers
Up/Down from last month #_____

_____ # of Email Opens (if known)
Up/Down from last month #_____

plan ahead

One class, seminar or webinar you'll attend in the next 2 months:
_____

One technique or technical skill you will improve or master next month:
_____

One thing you resolve to change in your work or personal life next month:

_____

_____

Verbal Merchandising

How you present your merchandise verbally (whether referring to products, your skills, your experience—anything that you want the client to accept or 'buy') **is one of the most powerful forms of merchandising you have.**

What other form of merchandising is more important than the words of someone who is an expert at handling and using a product, who understands the benefits it provides, the quality of its ingredients, secondary benefits like SPF protection, vitamins and anti-oxidants or aroma-therapeutic traits—what piece of literature or signage, what counter top display or shelf talker is more powerful than your words? Nothing!

A lot of stylists don't want to talk to clients about products because they worry they're going to sound like a salesperson. But think of it like this:

It's like you're trying to teach a cooking class and you also happen to carry all of the ingredients needed for each recipe for sale in your business. But because you are afraid to sound like a salesman, you don't tell your students what you are putting into the mix.

As crazy as that sounds, isn't that what you are doing when you create a look that the client loves, **but don't tell them exactly which products and tools they need to 'make it' at home** themselves?

Maybe you are not afraid to dialogue with your clients about products, but you really believe (and justifiably so) that your clients are in your care to escape and relax for a moment of personal indulgence, and that talking about products disrupts the experience.

Whatever is holding you back, you have to realize that until your customers hear and truly believe the depth of your convictions when it comes to the products you choose for them, based on your education and experience, they will not believe in them, either.

And if you withhold product endorsements, you appear ambivalent and neutral about the products you use. When the transfer of product knowledge is omitted from the customer experience, you leave the impression that products are an *un*important component of their overall experience.

Yes, they know you used shampoo and conditioner at the back bar. And they know that you emulsified something in your hands and then applied it to their hair prior to blow drying. And then you used something else when you pieced out their bangs, just before you sprayed some sort of finishing shine or holding product that had a great fragrance compared to what they are using at home. Your customers might have noticed fragrances and bottle colors...

...and when they are standing at the drug store trying to find **similar products to use** to recreate their look **at home,** they will try really hard to do a good job **picking out replacements.**

Why are they at the drug store? Because you did not tell them what was special about the products you used—you remember, those products you spent thousands of dollars to obtain and invested hundreds of hours to learn how, when and why to use them.

Now that you are convinced and ready to start showing off your products, remember that your merchandising, too, **must be done from a client-centric point of view.**

This means more than telling a client what you used, it means communicating specifically how a product benefits **the client,** how it fulfills a need of **the client,** how it meets a desire of **the client**. Any messaging that does not speak to the wants, needs, and good of **the client** is a wasted message.

To help you get started speaking the language of benefits, review the manufacturer and distributor literature you received this month. How much of the language speaks about the specific benefits products bring to the client? This is the language you can use in your salon signage and on your social media, internet and email marketing.

Merchandising How-To

The Retailer's Advantage (www.theretailorsadvantage.com) published a list by Rick Segel in January 2009 of the Top 12 Visual Merchandising Tips, and I've adapted it for salon and spa:

1. **Work from the outside, in.** Use what is visible from outside of your business (sidewalk or traffic areas, doorway, windows, etc.) to draw people in to your business. Create excitement, buzz, intrigue; spark a sense of curiosity about what is inside.

2. **Set the mood from the outside, in.** How do you want your customers to feel when they are inside your salon or spa? Begin to create ambiance, set the mood and create customer's expectations as to what will happen once they come inside. By the way, this does not only mean from the outside of the physical location of your salon or spa; you should begin to set the mood and create expectations with your web site, email and direct marketing pieces.

3. **Identify everything.** Customers are in a hurry. Every retail environment they enter is packed with items; some of which are relevant to their lives but go unnoticed because customers cannot see through the clutter to what is important. So identify everything. Use signage, color and displays to point out what is what. Tell people what they need to solve specific problems, and suggest additional items after you have their attention.

4. **Embrace all of the senses.** Setting the mood, stimulating curiosity and fully engaging customers in each client experience involves appealing to more than just the eyes when it comes to merchandising. Sounds, scents, how your products feel, sensations at the back bar and in the chair, the overall "atmosphere" created by your décor, the energy and attitude created by your staff—all of these beyond-visual components contribute to your overall client experience.

5. **Show customers how products will look in their home**, how a makeover would transform them, how to envision your products or gift cards as part of gifts for their friends and family. Help them visualize ownership or gift-giving.

6. **Group like with like.** Include displays where products that would/should normally be purchased together are grouped together. If your client needs a dry scalp shampoo, then they probably also need a moisturizing conditioner and soothing styling products.

7. **Group by lifestyle**. Sun worshipers? Pet owners? Foot fetishes? Group products together on displays that cater to the hobbies, activities and obsessions of your clients.

8. **Use the spotlight.** Light attracts the eye. This is why they use up-lights and spotlights in museums, galleries and other settings—to draw the eye to those things we most want people to focus on.

9. **Change. Displays. Often.** People get bored easily and we stop looking at things when we feel we have seen it before. Our minds tell us it's not new information and we do not need to pay close attention. Conversely, when we enter a familiar place that has been rearranged, renovated or significantly redecorated, we stop and look again, pausing to see items set apart with color and light, those things which surprise and delight us.

10. **Don't be afraid of color.** Just as with the use of light, use color to draw the eye to what is most important. And just as in the last tip, color groupings also need to change so that people don't stop looking at them. Seasonal events, holidays and promotions can help to inspire palettes or you can use background colors which make your products and gifts 'pop' in contrast to get attention.

11. **Integrate motion.** Motion attracts the eye and can demands immediate attention. When it comes to drawing attention to displays, you can use items that have integrated motion or you can even use items that move due to airflow from your HVAC, the opening of doors, even simple foot traffic like feathers, bubbles, sun catchers, etc.

12. **Remember the rule of 3.** Working in sets of 3's can help you to create displays that take the eye on a visual journey. Work at 3 heights (tall, taller, tallest) or widths (wide, wider, widest) in order to keep the eyes moving along a trajectory, along a set of messages, or a grouping of products. Or use (at least) 3 items of the same color to create a strong focal point; use of color to help unify your displays can be especially important if you have a lot of small-scale merchandise.

Use holidays, observances and themes as the basis to connect, engage and educate your prospects (aka "future clients") and current customers.

Finding Your Niche

Discovering your own strengths and passions and carving out your own professional "niche" should be where you invest **the most** in your own development.

Why? Even though trying to be 'everything' to 'everyone' isn't possible or desirable, it's a trap many people fall into. In most cases, the result is bland and boring for everyone, including you and your customers.

Finding your niche, on the other hand, those skills and customer-types you most enjoy and are best at working with, is where you will be **most profitable** as a stylist. Dedicating time developing and working in these are areas can set you apart from other stylists, help you create word-of-mouth buzz and enhance your professional reputation.

Selecting niche markets to cater to also gives you the ability to penetrate a saturated market. You won't be trying to do the same thing as everyone else; instead, you'll be better than most (if not the best) at something your ideal client types want most.

Finding your niche is a two-dimensional project and involves both inward and outward analysis:

Inside: Part of finding your niche involves knowing 'who' you are: deciding how you will be unique and identifying all the unique characteristics and strengths that (1) set you apart from others and which (2) are desired by your customers and ideal client types.

Outside: The other aspect involves identifying both the types of people your specialties are (1) likely to attract and (2) the types of people you want to attract, and then creating strategies to do so.

Identifying the types of people you are likely and most want to attract as clients gives you the ability to engage in target (or niche) marketing and this is where you should receive the highest return on your marketing investment.

Zeroing in on 'who' you want to attract gives you the ability to tailor messages specific enough to really get the attention of your target market. It also gives you the ability to put your marketing messages directly in the path of your target market, because you will be able to predict the places where they live, where else they shop or receive other types of services, what they do for entertainment, where they go to school or church, etc.

August 9 - Book Lovers Day

- Compile a list of favorite books to recommend to clients. Not a reader? Ask clients to help you create this list by sharing their favorite book titles.

- Hold a fundraiser or donate a portion of August retail sales to a local school library, a public library or a children's literacy program.

August 12-18 - National Smile Week

- Create a perfect smile kit with great shades of lipgloss and lipstick. Hold a lipstick demo or create a lipstick/cosmetics step-by-step to help clients create the perfect smile.

- Hold a contest via your website, Facebook page, blog, and in-salon, soliciting pictures for the "best smile."

- Create an online gallery with before-and-after photos that demonstrate your skills and/or how your services put smiles on your client's faces.

August 15 - National Relaxation Day

Put the spotlight on the products or services you provide that reduce stress or help with relaxation. Post info about aromatherapy on your social media, blog and email newsletter, highlighting products you carry that offer aromatherapy benefits.

August 19-25 - Resurrect Romance Week

- Write a Top 10 list of ways to resurrect romance to post on your website, email newsletter, blog and Facebook page. Weave your own romance-resurrecting products or services into the list.

- Post lists of romantic quotes, ways to propose, ways to ask someone to prom, romantic books or movies, etc., on Twitter, Facebook, blog and email newsletter.

- Solicit romantic stories about how people met, first dates, engagements, weddings or anniversaries on via your email newsletter and on Facebook and Twitter.

August 23 - Weird Contest Day

Create a weird contest or solicit weird contest ideas from customers and implement one or more of the winning suggestions.

 Facebook Twitter Blog Email/Mail

August

Sunday	Monday	Tuesday	Wednesday	Thursday	Friday	Saturday
			✉ f t **1** Send August email newsletter and offers	f t **2**	**3**	**4**
5	**6**	f t **7**	**8**	**9** **Book Lovers Day**	📶 f t **10**	**11**
12	**13** **National Smile Week August 12-18**	f t **14** Look ahead! Finalize September details and plan Oct. and Nov.	**15** **National Relaxation Day**	f t **16**	**17**	**18**
19	**20** **Resurrect Romance Week August 19-25**	✉ f t **21** Send email: August 'Last Chance!' and Sept/Oct preview	**22**	**23** **Weird Contest Day**	📶 f t **24**	**25**
26	**27**	f t **28** Take/break down expired promotions; set up for September	**29**	**30**	f t **31**	**A smile is a curve that sets everything straight.** (Phyllis Diller)

score card

Check one box for every communication task completed from the above calendar this month:

week one
☐ ☐ ☐ ☐ ☐

week two
☐ ☐ ☐ ☐

week three
☐ ☐ ☐

week four
☐ ☐ ☐ ☐ ☐

week five
☐ ☐ ☐

_____ # of **New Clients**
Up/Down from last month #_____

_____ # of **Retail Products** sold
Up/Down from last month #_____

 _____ # of Facebook Fans/Friends
Up/Down from last month #_____

 _____ # of Twitter Followers
Up/Down from last month #_____

📶 _____ # of Blog Hits/Readers
Up/Down from last month #_____

✉ _____ # of Email Subscribers
Up/Down from last month #_____

_____ # of Email Opens (if known)
Up/Down from last month #_____

plan ahead

One class, seminar or webinar you'll attend in the next 2 months:
_____

One technique or technical skill you will improve or master next month:
_____

One thing you resolve to change in your work or personal life next month:
_____
_____

Finding your Niche: The Brand of You

We have all heard snippets of the popular "You Might Be a Redneck…" series of one-liner jokes by Jeff Foxworthy, with such gems as "If you've been married three times, and you always had the same in-laws, you might be a redneck."

No matter where you grew up, or how polished your family, you have likely identified with one or more of the statements (or are closely related to someone who does!)

The same principles apply to you. If you slink in late with unwashed hair in a ponytail and dare your boss to comment, you might have "just a job." If you forget your client's name three minutes into a consultation, if you don't bother to rebook, if you never suggest retail products for home use, and if you would rather "eyeball" your color mixture than measure it, you might have "just a job" (and you might not have that one for long).

If all you want is a job, and all you need is a paycheck, skip the rest of this guide. An out-of-work once-friend begged me to help them find a job–well, sort of. They actually said, "I don't want a job, I want an income," and asked me to hook them up with get-rich-quick internet opportunities.

While a few people do "get rich quick," in most cases they do so only after spending years developing their craft, doing research, learning the ropes, and working hard.

> I know you didn't get in to this business for the marketing part of the job.

You may have had a short introduction to marketing as part of your schooling, but you were probably more interested in learning your craft, developing your technique, and making art than you were about the mechanics of marketing.

> But marketing yourself is essential in a sea of sameness.

No matter how talented you are or how well you treat your clients, there are other people who "do what you do."

Marketing includes activities that you do in order to persuade people that you do what you do in a way that is better artistically and better for them as a client, than others in your profession. Marketing is giving clients reasons and opportunities to choose you. As a new stylist, you are entering a professional world where your peers already have established clientele. Among your most important responsibilities is not only what you do behind the chair — it is to build your client base, and that will require knowing the brand of "you" so that you can effectively market yourself as a stylist.

> Don't get me wrong, what you do behind the chair matters a great deal when it comes to building your client base.

> But you can't do 'what you do' behind the chair if no one is sitting in it!

Creating the Brand of You

Like it or not, you have a brand. Brand You is built in the mind of your customers and prospects every time they come into contact with you or with anyone who is talking about you.

Everything they experience with you directly, and everything that they hear about you gets bundled up in their brain and forms Brand You in their mind.

And just like a business would, you can dedicate time to developing a strong, consistent brand:

- What is your personal mission statement? What do you do for your clients? What do you do better than others or love most?

- What is your vision—the greater good you want to do in the world through your choice of profession?

- How do you present yourself to the world? Do you think through your own outward appearance in terms of style and dress so that the positive things you want people to believe about you are established and reinforced in the minds of your customers, prospects, peers—anyone who might be talking about you to others?

Niche Markets

Extras

In August, children across the US get ready to go back to school.

If your ideal clients can be found amongst school employees or students, their teachers and/or parents, then reaching out to market yourself to the back-to-school crowd makes good sense!

Here are 10 ways to reach out to this market:

1. Hold an educators open house featuring easy-maintenance, current hair and makeup styles for teachers.

   Send a copy of your event invitation to the offices of local schools. Include pictures of stylish easy-to-manage hair and makeup looks in your email newsletter and on Facebook and ask clients to bring in pictures of the looks that they want for the school year.

2. Hold a back-to-school hairstyle and makeup show for students and their parents; solicit volunteers to model youth-trendy hair styles, makeup, etc.

   Teach attendees how to recreate trendy looks at home and extend event-only offers that include the tools and products needed.

3. Throughout the year, use photos featuring younger celebrities or models to help you make suggestions and to stimulate conversations about trendy cuts and styles.

   Include them on your email newsletter and social media. Talk about the products and tools needed to create the looks at home.

4. Do you have clients whose kids receive their services somewhere else? Extend special multi-booking appointment times so parents can bring all their kids in at the same time at a family rate.

   Offer to rebook the whole family 6 weeks later (or 3 weeks later for the guys) together, at the same rate.

5. As you do back-to-school haircuts on kids this month, tell parents about scalp, hair or skin issues you see and write up 'prescriptions' for recommended reparative products as well as how to use them.

6. Consider extending a special, on-going offer just for teachers, such as a break on retail purchased at appointments, or a free retail product for every third haircut, etc. Create a refer-a-teacher reward.

7. Promote the giving of your gift certificates and your best-selling products (like serums, shine products, aroma-therapeutic lotions, etc.) as gifts for teachers all year long.

   Plan now to create special gift sets designed as holiday gifts for teachers, and begin marketing these early in November. Be sure each gift set includes your business card, menu of services, and new client (or teacher) offer.

8. Create a school year desk or wall calendar to give to all your clients that includes a product or service of the month spotlight as well as a monthly promotion for the spotlighted item.

9. Create a school year booklet that features teacher-only special offers for each month of the school year and send copies in bulk to offices of local private and public schools, and school district offices.

10. Inquire with your local public and private schools about opportunities to advertise in school newsletters and the school yearbook, to donate to school auctions, to be a 'booster' for sport teams or provide support for choirs, orchestras, dramas or other arts programs, to support literacy or after school programs, etc.

Use holidays, observances and themes as the basis to connect, engage and educate your prospects (aka "future clients") and current customers.

Niche Marketing that should be
Music to Your Ears

Your community as a whole is made up of many different mini-communities—people connected by family, friends, common interests, hobbies, entertainment, sports and by so many other circumstantial means.

Here are 9 ways to reach out to musicians and music teachers in your community to help build your business:

- Partner with local music studios and piano teachers for cross marketing. Create special offers just for music teachers or create special offers which teachers or music stores can pass on to their students and patrons.

- Hold a contest or drawing, taking nominations for the best area music teachers, and reward one of more of these with a gift card and pampering product reward. After the contest, use email or direct mail to extend a special offer to all nominees and to those who nominated them.

- Tell music students in your community about the benefits your most pampering services for themselves or what a great gift it would make for their music teachers.

- Create a gift basket with gift card and pampering products and a favorite music album or a musical movie and promote it to clients as a gift for music teachers, dance instructors and other music professionals.

- Add pre-recital and pre-performance hair color, styling, manicure and/or makeup services to your menu.

- Add post-performance de-stressing massages, manicures, pedicures or other services to your menu.

- Set aside space on your website or in email marketing to help promote local school, amateur or professional concerts, recitals and musicals. Help promote ticket sales.

- Create a gift basket with gift card and pampering products and a favorite music album or a musical movie and promote it to clients as a gift for music teachers, dance instructors and other music professionals.

September 6 – Truancy Prevention Day

Here's a back-to-school marketing theme you probably never thought of: Help prevent truancy.

- Design a perfect attendance pledge form for students to sign at the beginning of the year. Reward students who achieve perfect attendance at the end of the school year.

- Establish a rewards program where students accrue points for attendance, good grades, scholastic and other accomplishments throughout the year.

September 11 – Grandparents Day

- Solicit stories about grandparents on your blog or Facebook page. Ask people to share the best advice or funniest one-liners their grandparents used to say.

- Suggest specific services and products as ideal gifts for grandparents or seniors.

- Work with local senior living communities to coordinate transport to your business for appointments. Set aside senior appointment or shopping hours or extend a senior citizen discount.

September 21 – World Gratitude Day

If you are not in the habit of writing thank-you notes to **at least** your most **loyal or valuable clients**, start today. Commit to writing at least one thank-you note every day; write one to each client, if possible.

September 27 – Love Note Day

- Distribute 'love notes' to your customers on bag stuffers, business cards or receipts. Print them as part of receipts, include them in your email newsletter or mail postcards or letters to customers.

- Ask customers to write a 'love note' about their favorite product or service to be used as a testimonial or review in your email newsletters and on social media.

September 28 – Ask a Stupid Question Day

Asking questions can be a great way to stimulate sales—and that's never stupid! Put 'Frequently Asked Questions' (FAQ) and their answers on Facebook, your blog, email newsletter and bag stuffers that address common nail, skin or hair problems.

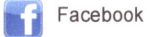 Facebook   Twitter   Blog  Email/Mail

September

Sunday	Monday	Tuesday	Wednesday	Thursday	Friday	Saturday
						1
2	3 **Labor Day**	4 Send September email newsletter and offers	5	6 **Truancy Prevention Day**	7	8
9	10	11 **Grandparents Day**	12	13	14	15
16	17	18 Look ahead! Finalize Oct. details and plan Nov. and Dec.	19	20	21 **World Gratitude Day**	22 **First Day of Autumn**
23	24 Set aside time to plan for the holiday season	25 Send email: Sept. 'Last Chance!' and Oct/Nov preview	26	27 **Love Note Day**	28 **Ask a Stupid Question Day**	29 Take/break down expired promotions; set up for October
30				Time, which changes people, does not alter the image we have retained of them. (Marcel Proust)		

score card

Check one box for every communication task completed from the above calendar this month:

week one
☐ ☐ ☐ ☐ ☐

week two
☐ ☐ ☐ ☐ ☐

week three
☐ ☐ ☐ ☐

week four
☐ ☐ ☐ ☐ ☐ ☐

_____# of **New Clients**
Up/Down from last month #_____

_____# of **Retail Products** sold
Up/Down from last month #_____

_____# of Facebook Fans/Friends
Up/Down from last month #_____

_____# of Twitter Followers
Up/Down from last month #_____

_____# of Blog Hits/Readers
Up/Down from last month #_____

_____# of Email Subscribers
Up/Down from last month #_____

_____# of Email Opens (if known)
Up/Down from last month #_____

plan ahead

One class, seminar or webinar you'll attend in the next 2 months:
_____

One technique or technical skill you will improve or master next month:
_____

One thing you resolve to change in your work or personal life next month:
_____
_____

The Power of 'Thank You'

Sometimes we behave as though **we believe clients should be thanking us** for the services we provide (in exchange for money) to them.

The reality is, **we should be thanking them** for their patronage, the first time and every time. Your clients have lots of choices; in fact, there may literally be hundreds of other stylists or estheticians in your city they could choose to patronize.

Note cards, and specifically thank you notes, postcards or even thank-you business cards (maybe with a great inspirational quote on it) should be one of the staples of your personal marketing toolbox; one that you use **daily**.

Personal notes may be one of the most underrated forms of marketing when it comes to brand and relationship building even though it is one of the easiest to implement.

Once you get the hang of writing a quick note to someone, it won't seem like such a chore. It will be uplifting for you to remember the high points of your day and extend a word of encouragement to others.

Beyond the 'thank you,' here are some of the events that might trigger a note from you to a client, co-worker, vendor, consultant, friend, etc.:

- To say goodbye to a client who is moving away, going off to college or leaving on a military deployment (or to encourage a military spouse or parent)
- In sympathy or to say that you're thinking of someone due to the death of a loved one, job loss, divorce or separation, etc.
- To encourage someone who had a bad day

- As a personal invitation to an upcoming event or promotion
- Included as a note of congratulations with a special offer in your gift or charity auction baskets
- Congratulations for events such as a new baby, new job, promotion, new home, new marriage or engagement, graduation, awards, accomplishments, marathons, significant weight loss or other self-improvement
- 'Thinking of you' or 'miss you' notes to clients you have not seen in more than 60 days
- As a thank you to your children's teachers, or as a thank you to the principal or other leaders of local schools or district offices
- As a thank you to your business marketing partners, businesses near you and/ or those who participate in cross or cooperative marketing with you
- As a get well / feel better soon, or other card of encouragement
- To extend employee appreciation, compliments or kudos
- As a note to city hall, a local politician or civic leader
- To communicate with the owners of local businesses
- As a thank you to local charity organizations, animal shelters, community services or volunteers
- As a thank you to someone who made your day, to a co-worker, or to a client for loyalty or referral
- As a thank you / new client welcome
- Holidays—Christmas, Thanksgiving, New Year, Valentine's Day, etc.
- To acknowledge milestones such as birthdays and anniversaries

September is Build a Better Image Month

In contrast to self-improvement, which often involves changes we make on the inside, building a better image is about how we appear to others—and "branding" is how your build your image.

Your image, or brand, is—essentially—**a promise** that exists **in the customer's mind** about **who you are** and **the benefits you provide** that gets reinforced **every single time** they come into contact with you.

Building a better image is about putting the stamp of the personality, values, culture, beliefs—the very essence of what you really want your client's experience to be—on every possible customer touch point.

Why is this important?

Without a strong brand image in the client's mind, you have to build a case for why you **DESERVE** their business, **every single time** you get ready to make a sale.

Businesses with strong brands are closing deals while others are still introducing themselves.

In August's Extras, we talked about some of the elements you need to understand and develop in order to have a strong personal brand. When it comes to your business, it's important that you have an understanding of the basic elements of what is called "Brand Identity."

Brand identity is made up of the visual and verbal icons and words that you choose to represent your business.

September Extras

Here are the **3 most common** elements of a business's **brand identity**:

Vision Statement

IS NOT: what you are going to do or how you are going to do it

IS: what your organization ultimately aspires to become, will resonate with customers and employees, will make everyone connected to your business feel proud, excited and that they are part of something bigger than themselves. Your vision is the good that your company will ultimately provide to the world. It explains why you are doing what you are doing and the good that success will enable your business to accomplish.

Mission Statement

IS NOT: about you, is not fluffy, ethereal or esoteric

IS: a definition of why you (deserve to) exist; a precise description of what you do; should describe the business you are in. Your mission statement should give your employees a clear idea of how their role helps fulfill the vision. Your mission statement is the practical route or means you will employ to achieve your vision.

Tagline, Motto or Slogan

IS: your promise. The promise that guides the development of your business strategies and all the elements of your brand. It's a word, short phrase or single sentence that explains how you benefit your customer in a meaningful, impactful way.

Express Train to Success

Use holidays, observances and themes as the basis to connect, engage and educate your prospects (aka "future clients") and current customers.

Express Train to Success

Many people are looking for the express train (if you will) to success, but most don't like the answer when they hear it, because, as Thomas Edison said, "It's dressed in overalls and it looks like work."

While we all dream of having one great idea, genius breakthrough or another ticket to overnight success, 99.9% of the time, that's not where we're going to find it. There are things successful people have in common, but they can only be achieved over time:

Strong performance.

This is about your reputation and track record over time in not only fulfilling your responsibilities but also by consistently exceeding expectations and goals. This isn't about doing what's expected, it's about doing more than what's expected, most of the time.

Ethics.

This is about who you really are on the inside coming out on the outside. You can discover that person in the actions and behaviors you engage in when (you think) no one else is looking. How about the little things – do you show up on time, every time? Stretch your lunch break? Do personal tasks on the clock? Shirk cleaning duties? And how about your personal appearance – do you ride the line of what's appropriate or allowed in the workplace, or do you dress for the position you aspire to achieve?

Drive.

You demonstrate drive when you show up, day in and day out, ready to go. You demonstrate drive when you take on responsibilities outside of the scope of your job and complete them, with style and enthusiasm. You demonstrate drive when you seek out continuing education at every opportunity.

And that brings me to one last point:
To get where you want to go in your professional career, be the sidekick.

Seek out mentors and take in all that they're willing to teach you. Be observant and take note of what sets successful people apart from others; not only what they know or can do, but how they treat others, what they value and what they think is most important.

October 9 - Curious Events Day

- Post 'curious events' on Twitter, Facebook, bag stuffers, station talkers, your blog and email newsletter.

- Write the story of why you became a stylist as a sequence of curious events and release the story post by post on Facebook, include it on your blog and email newsletters.

- Put "Did you know...?" style posts about your industry, products, services, city, local leaders, celebrities—anything your customers would be especially curious about—in posts on Twitter, Facebook, bag stuffers, your blog and email newsletter.

- Write marketing copy and social media posts in such a way that your audience is teased – *curious* and intrigued enough so that they simply have to know more, try a product, experience a service or come to your business to see what's new.

October 18 - Make a Difference Day

Another marketing term you should become familiar with is "Unique Selling Proposition" or USP (also known as unique value proposition). Your personal USP is what sets you apart from other stylists. These are the same niche skills that you identified and determined to continue developing that will differentiate you from competitors in order to help you get more clients, develop loyalty among your customers and give you an edge when it comes to professional advancement. Here are some elements to think about when you are looking for your own USP:

- What differentiates you from your peers?

- What is special about the products and/or services you provide; how do they benefit your customers or members of your prime target markets?

- What are the benefits to the customer of doing business with you and/or how do you improve their lives?

October 25 - Knock Knock Jokes Day

Feature the phrase "Knock, knock!" in big block lettering at the top of a posters, displays, door hangers, emails, newsletters or the front of postcards—it's sure to grab attention. Write marketing messages that begin with "Knock, knock! Who's there?" and answer the question in a fun way to draw attention to products or services that solve common customer needs.

 Facebook    Twitter   Blog    Email/Mail

Sunday	Monday	Tuesday	Wednesday	Thursday	Friday	Saturday
		1 ✉ f t 2 **Send October email newsletter and offers**	3	4 f t	5	6
7	8 **Columbus Day**	f t 9 **Curious Events Day**	10	11	📶 f t 12	13
14	15	f t 16 **Look ahead! Finalize Nov. details and plan Dec. and Jan.**	17	18 f t 19 **Make a Difference Day**		20
21	22	✉ f t 23 **Send email: Oct. 'Last Chance!' and Nov/Dec preview**	24	25 📶 f t 26 **Knock Knock Jokes Day**		27
28	29	f t 30	31 **Halloween**	Take/break down expired promotions; set up for November	**You cannot do a kindness too soon, for you never know how soon it will be too late.** (Ralph Waldo Emerson)	

score card

Check one box for every communication task completed from the above calendar this month:

week one
☐ ☐ ☐ ☐ ☐

week two
☐ ☐ ☐ ☐ ☐

week three
☐ ☐ ☐ ☐

week four
☐ ☐ ☐ ☐ ☐ ☐

week five
☐ ☐

_____# of **New Clients**
Up/Down from last month #_____

_____# of **Retail Products** sold
Up/Down from last month #_____

f _____# of Facebook Fans/Friends
Up/Down from last month #_____

t _____# of Twitter Followers
Up/Down from last month #_____

📶 _____# of Blog Hits/Readers
Up/Down from last month #_____

✉ _____# of Email Subscribers
Up/Down from last month #_____

_____# of Email Opens (if known)
Up/Down from last month #_____

plan ahead

One class, seminar or webinar you'll attend in the next 2 months:

_____

One technique or technical skill you will improve or master next month:

_____

One thing you resolve to change in your work or personal life next month:

_____
_____

6 Ways Your Business Cards Can
Make You Money

We think of business cards as essential to doing business in the modern world (and they are).

But you may not know that **business cards** have been around for **hundreds of years**, and they've always been **important.**

Business cards were originally used by the most prosperous and the aristocratic in society to announce that they would be coming to town soon, were exchanged during introductions and were left at the homes of peers and friends to note that one had stopped by.

It's amazing, if you think about it, that we still use business cards in what is – essentially – the same way. We use them to introduce ourselves, we send them with collateral, we leave them at other businesses, we hand them out at events and parties.

Business cards might be the most often-used tool in your marketing arsenal; yet it's often given little attention in terms of design. Worse, many times people hand out business cards that contain obsolete or outdated information, crossing out and writing in new data. This sends all kinds of negative messages; that you're careless, that you don't care how you present yourself, that you're not proud of your business, that you're not successful enough to be able to afford to replenish them (and who wants to work with someone who is unsuccessful at what they do?)

Since it's the job of your business card to introduce you to others and remind people of your existence, your business cards need to be memorable, need to reflect your brand and the personality of your business, must look professional and must be kept up to date.

Once you've got this tool ready to work, **here are 6 ways** to use your business cards to **make money:**

1. Don't leave home without them. Sounds obvious, doesn't it, but how many times have you been at a party, a store, somewhere and in the middle of a conversation with someone, you have an opportunity to give them your contact information but find yourself without a card?

If it was good enough for the rich and famous for hundreds of years, it's good enough for you, too! Give away your business cards to people to whom you are introduced or meet at networking and social events. Introduce yourself to the managers or owners of businesses you visit on a regular basis and leave two copies of your card with them (one to give away).

2. Include 2 business cards (one to give away) in each Thank-You Note you send. Which of course implies that you are, in fact, thanking your customers. All of your customers. Your most important clients. Your most loyal patrons. (Come on, you can thank at least one person each day, can't you?)

3. Send your business cards to large employers or organizations in your area for placement in common areas, like break rooms. Create a special offer and have it printed on your cards. Send or (better yet) hand-deliver a gift basket with product samples, treats and your service menu to the receptionist, human resources department, etc; introduce yourself, note the special offer you're extending and ask that your cards be placed in lobbies, break, lunch or other common areas. Provide digital ad copy that can be featured in their newsletters or on their employee/member websites.

4. Place your business cards strategically throughout your building on displays. Draw attention to special offers, departmental features, awards or charity involvement, etc.

5. Include business cards with products, services or gift certificates that you donate to non-profit fundraising drives, auctions, etc. When you donate, ask that your business cards be placed near your auction basket or featured in printed or online collateral.

6. Create a digital version of your business card that can be downloaded from your website, blog or email newsletter and easily shared with others. Put information about your new customer offers or referral rewards on your digital business card.

Bonus #7: Give your business cards and/or special offer out with Halloween Treats from your business or even from your home.

October is
Customer Service Month

According to a 2011 American Express Global Customer Service Barometer (a survey done in the USA and 9 other countries relative to attitudes and preferences toward customer service), **70%** of Americans said they would be willing to **spend almost 15% more** with businesses they believed (really) provided excellent customer service. You would think that businesses would make customer service a top priority; but in the same survey, 60% of respondents said **they don't believe businesses are making customer service a high priority.** In fact, 26% said they think businesses are actually paying less attention to service.

A lot of people simply don't understand what customer service 'is,' or maybe they misinterpret or fail to deliver what it is their customers really want.

The real question is, what **about** your customer service is surprising or remarkable – *soooooooo* **extraordinary** that clients walk out the door and are compelled to tell other people about it? If you can't pinpoint how the customer service you provide to clients, day in and day out, is truly outside of what they expect, then it's probably not exceptional.

I would argue that most of what occurs in the vast majority of salons and spas merely falls within customer expectations. They expect to be treated like guests. They expect to receive great services and buy products that do what you promised. They expect you to be cheerful and helpful. They expect you to be knowledgeable about your work, your products, new techniques and trends.

So even if you do **all these things,** you're doing no more than **meeting** your client's **basic expectations**. There is nothing exceptional about simply meeting expectations!

According to Wikipedia.org, "**Customer Service is the provision of services to customers before, during and after a purchase,**" so far, so good, there's not much there to change the basic understanding held by most people. But the description goes on to reference Efraim Turban's 2002 book, "Electronic Commerce: A Managerial Perspective" where he says that customer service is **"a series of activities designed to enhance the level of customer satisfaction — that is,** *the feeling* **that a product or service has met the customer expectation."**

October
Extras

Whoa—that's a whole different take! According to this line of thinking, the definition of customer service is not contained in the actions of a person taking a phone order, fulfilling a web order, receiving a return or complaint, performing a service or selling a product. Customer service isn't an action, it's a process—an intentionally designed system—meant to enhance the customer's experience and which influences *whether a customer feels* satisfied or dissatisfied by a product or service.

A sales transaction, product or service on its own is not enough to produce customer satisfaction. You must systematically examine and strategically improve each and every aspect of the customer experience, at every possible touch point. You must create a system designed to enhance the customer experience. Do you know what that really means? According to thefreedictionary.com,

en-hance (verb) means:

1) **to make greater, as in value, beauty, or effectiveness; to augment**

2) **to provide with improved, advanced or sophisticated features**

It's not just about making the customer experience "better." It's about making it greater in value, bigger (augmented) and/or more sophisticated—**more than that of the competition** and **more than the customer expects**—so that it stands out *to the customer.*

If you wonder why people don't always agree with the claim you make that you provide "exceptional customer service" or why the customer experience you demonstrate is **not** helping you gain and retain clients, it's because **what you have in place** is not actually enough to influence the customer to *feel* **exceptionally satisfied**. It may technically be "good enough" but if it's not **more than expected** and doesn't **set you apart from the competition**, it's not good enough!

Use holidays, observances and themes as the basis to connect, engage and educate your prospects (aka "future clients") and current customers.

Put your Clients in the Hammock

Close your eyes and breathe deeply and slowly, in and out, exhaling completely 10 times. With your eyes still closed, imagine yourself somewhere warm but not hot, with just the hint of a breeze blowing across your body as you lay in the sun, swinging slowly back and forth in a hammock over a white sandy beach, the sound of the ocean in your ears.

Unworried, far from the cares of life and free of the demands you make on yourself and those required of you by others. Content, perfectly satisfied with yourself and your surroundings, wanting for nothing, alone or with the perfect companion—whatever suits your fantasy best.

Why? This is the level of experience you should want to create for your clients. One they can count on every few weeks when they will be able to step away from all the things that they have to do and will have a chance to just be:

You want your clients "in the hammock."

Think about the type of atmosphere you want to create, and then design the client experience from end to end. Because these are the support posts and netting that holds your client hammock in place. Loose netting or weak posts will put clients at constant risk of falling out of the hammock—falling out of the experience you want to create.

Make a list of all of the variables that comprise your client experience, from the moment they arrive, to the reception and waiting area, through each area they might touch during their appointment, through to the end of their visit and even what will happen after they leave.

Think about background elements like music, lighting, decor, cleanliness. Re-design touch points with the goal of reinforcing the atmosphere you want to create for each and every customer, and map out a plan to transform each, one by one, over the coming months.

Think about personal comfort such as hunger, thirst or need of a rest room (especially during longer appointments). Use scripts so that every customer will be received hospitably and treated as a pampered guest.

November 2 - Look for Circles Day

Fill a large glass container with marbles, rubber balls, gum balls—any circular item will do—and have customers guess the quantity. Post a picture online so people can enter on Facebook and Twitter or by responding via email. Use entries to build your contact database and extend a special offer to all entrants.

November 8 - Set a Record, Do a Stunt Day

- And November 13th is Guinness Book of World Records Day. Set a new world record or hold a publicity stunt on your own or with marketing partners. Solicit ideas and participation from customers, co-workers, marketing partners, and/or the general public.

- Post links to interesting world records or the official Guinness Book site on Twitter, Facebook, bag stuffers, your blog and email newsletter. Draw attention to recent or historical local records and stunts.

November 16 - Button Day

- Wear "Ask me about..." buttons (and/or similar signage for shelving, waiting area, the point of purchase, etc.) to encourage clients to ask about new products or services, add-ons or time-limited promotions. Write "Did you know...?" posts for Twitter, Facebook, your blog and email newsletter to get the attention of readers talk about products and services.

- Add like and retweet buttons to blog posts to stimulate internet traffic and article sharing. Encourage readers to forward your emails and share your blog, Facebook and Twitter posts.

November 19 - Electronic Greeting Card Day

Send an electronic greeting card thanking clients for their patronage and wishing them a Happy Thanksgiving. Add an offer to your electronic greeting or a code word redeemable for a specific discount, free add-on, branded tchotchke, etc.

November 24 - World Hello Day

- Reach out personally to clients you have not seen in a while, or who have not rebooked at their regular frequency.

- Post "hello" in different languages on your Facebook page, blog and email newsletter. Share trivia about various cultural greeting traditions and taboos on social media and email.

November

Sunday	Monday	Tuesday	Wednesday	Thursday	Friday	Saturday
				📧 f t 1 Send November email newsletter and offers	f t 2 **Look for Circles Day**	3
4 **Daylight Saving Time Ends**	5	f t 6 **Election Day**	7	8 **Set a Record, Do a Stunt Day**	📶 f t 9	10
f t 11 **Veterans Day**	12 **Veterans Day (Observed)**	f t 13 Look ahead! Finalize Dec. details and plan Jan. and Feb. 2013	14	15	f t 16 **Button Day**	17
18	19 **Electronic Greeting Card Day**	📧 f t 20 Send email: November 'Last Chance!' and Dec/Jan preview	21	📧 f t 22 **Send a Thanksgiving e-greeting**	📶 f t 23 **Black Friday**	24 **World Hello Day & Small Business Saturday**
25	26 .Cyber Monday	f t 27	28	29	f t 30 Take/break down expired promotions; set up for December	**Gratitude is the sign of noble souls.** (Aesop)

score card

Check one box for every communication task completed from the above calendar this month:

week one
☐ ☐ ☐ ☐ ☐

week two
☐ ☐ ☐ ☐ ☐

week three
☐ ☐ ☐ ☐ ☐ ☐

week four
☐ ☐ ☐ ☐ ☐
☐ ☐ ☐

week five
☐ ☐ ☐ ☐

_____# of **New Clients**
Up/Down from last month #_____

_____# of **Retail Products** sold
Up/Down from last month #_____

 _____# of Facebook Fans/Friends
Up/Down from last month #_____

 _____# of Twitter Followers
Up/Down from last month #_____

 _____# of Blog Hits/Readers
Up/Down from last month #_____

 _____# of Email Subscribers
Up/Down from last month #_____

_____# of Email Opens (if known)
Up/Down from last month #_____

plan ahead

One class, seminar or webinar you'll attend in the next 2 months:

_____

One technique or technical skill you will improve or master next month:

_____

One thing you resolve to change in your work or personal life next month:

_____

_____

Using Fund Raising to Build Business

You can choose to support one or any number of charities in your community through themed promotions or events, but it may be more beneficial for you and for the charities you most want to support if you select just one or two organizations to support on a regular basis.

When considering your options, why not choose to benefit organizations that have directly impacted your own life?

You will express yourself the most honestly and persuasively when speaking to issues you understand personally. Plus, you will receive the most personal satisfaction when you help support causes you genuinely believe in.

One word of caution: if you don't genuinely desire to support a charitable cause, don't add one to your event. You can benefit your business while also benefitting a charity, but you should approach this idea with the goal of developing a long-term, on-going relationship with a specific charity or cause/s you truly want to benefit.

Here are some ways to benefit a charity while building business:

- Events or marketing promotions with all profits* going to charity (*net proceeds after costs)

- Events with **all** proceeds going to charity (costs are donated)

- Events with a cover charge going to charity

- Events or marketing promotions with a percentage of overall or specific product/service sales going to charity

- Solicit donations or a portion of sales and promise to match the donation up to a certain amount, or acquire a corporate or individual sponsor willing to match donations up to a certain amount

- Product or service of the month with proceeds or percentage of sales to charity (or a certain dollar amount for each unit sold, etc.)

- Feature information in your communications about your charity, its needs, and how it benefits others on an on-going basis to help build awareness, or as build up to a specific event or marketing promotion

- Donate actual products or services to a charity, to patients or their family members, to care givers, to the employees of the charity, etc.

- Hold a cut-a-thon, massage-a-thon, polish-a-thon, etc., accepting donations for the charity in lieu of payment for services and encouraging contributions from all clients, corporate sponsors, advertisers, etc.

- Treat someone in need to 'celebrity for a day' treatment

- Create a 'make over a hero' program where clients can nominate someone in the community who deserves some special pampering (and create bigger prize packages by working together with other businesses to create a bigger program)

- Adopt a family (or an individual) for a year or another specified time period, for a specific service, or for a series of services

However you decide to do the math after an event, remember that the more you whittle down the portion designated for charity, the more that it will appear that the event was held for you, not the charity. Hold yourself accountable by setting a minimum donation amount and by telling your clients, employees and marketing partners how much money was raised for the charity following your event or promotion.

In the weeks leading up to your event or promotion, send press releases to local newspapers, magazines, radio stations, local and national offices of the charity, city hall, and other media highlighting your chosen charity and the work that it does as well as how your event will benefit them.

- 6 weeks before event / promotion—send a general press release with "more to follow"

- 3-4 weeks before the event / promotion—send a second press release with more details and a compelling reason for people to support the charity and your event

- 1 week before the event / promotion—send a full press release

- Throughout the weeks leading to your event or promotion, use social media to tease, intrigue and inform your followers

- After the event / promotion—send a press release including one or two of the best photos and summary results

November
Extras

The 2nd Week of November is
National Hunger and Homeless Week

During the holiday season, use social media and your email newsletter to help raise awareness of the **needs** of local shelters, food banks, missions and similar **charitable food and housing providers.**

- Extend a special offer or give small thank-you gifts to clients who donate money, food, or clothing to these charities.

- Donate a portion of sales from product or service sales in November to a local charitable meal provider.

- Publicize efforts and raise awareness within your community in press releases submitted to local radio and news stations/reporters, local newspapers and city magazines.

- Posts statistics about the local hungry/homeless population on your Facebook page, blog and email newsletter.

- Post trivia such as the average cost per day needed to make a difference at local charities or ways that people can volunteer or provide personal assistance.

Ready for 2013? Go to www.12monthsofmarketing.net **for your 2013 marketing guide!**

November is Military Family Appreciation Month

Use your Facebook page, blog site and email to extend a special offer to local military members and their families or host a military family open house.

Send a copy of your offer to the newspaper of your local military base for inclusion in updates to military families, or send a stack of offer cards, business cards and/or your menu to the offices of military family service organizations.

'Adopt' a local member of the military (or a spouse) for free haircuts, massages, manicures or other services for a year.

If you do not live near a military base, extend a special offer to all Veterans in your community and take copies of your offer, business card, menu and manufacturer's samples to the office of your local V.A. (Veteran's Administration) or other Veteran's organization.

Host a holiday care package or holiday greeting card event and invite clients and community members to come and write a thank you note and solicit drawings from children, and/or solicit donations and gifts suitable for sending to troops overseas during the holidays.

Create military care package product baskets for retail sale containing a product mix perfect for military members based in dry, hot climates (like the Middle East) or other typical military environs. Include foil packettes and other samples and products that will travel or ship well. Hold a contest and award one or two of the baskets for free as well as selling these in your retail mix.

Use holidays, observances and themes as the basis to connect, engage and educate your prospects (aka "future clients") and current customers.

Out with the Old...
In with the New

Prepare for the New Year, including putting the finishing touches on your 2013 marketing plan. Set aside time to take stock of where you are, how far you have come during the past year, and make New Year's Professional Resolutions. You might be planning to start or expand your business, become an educator, provide consulting services, enter a competition, publish your work, expand your product or service lines, it might be time to update your pricing, or to make other changes.

No matter what your goals, **putting them on paper and noting incremental steps** you'll need to take to reach them will help you avoid procrastinating.

Take the first (or next) step toward your goals. Share your goals and goal timeline with a trusted friend or mentor—this can be another way to help hold yourself accountable.

Measure and analyze the initiatives, marketing efforts, events, and marketing partnerships you did during the last 12 months against the goals set for each. Think about what else you learned—more than just whether you actually met your objective.

Take note of unexpected or indirect benefits or downsides: what worked well, what you enjoyed the most, which customers enjoyed most, which drew the most participation, which seemed to stimulate customer engagement, which employees enjoyed most (or least) or which garnered the most employee buy in (or resistance), those that had problems you had not anticipated or where you fell short in efforts to market, promote or create buzz around marketing activities.

Speak to key customers about what kinds of offers would induce them to take action or to refer friends and family to you for services. Asking loyal clients, trusted friends and/or co-workers to participate in focus groups, and getting feedback on a regular basis can help you construct more effective promotions and events, avoid unforeseen pitfalls and give clients what they really want as you try to build a bigger role for your business in their lives.

Use this information to make adjustments to your marketing plan for the coming year.

December 6 - Roof Over Your Head Day

- Does your business share a roof (mall, business park, etc.) with others? Work together to hold a special holiday open house, holiday hair and makeup demonstration or sale event.

- Extend special offers to employees or the customers of businesses that share a roof with you. Ask those businesses to display your offers, hand out bag stuffers and include your offers in newsletters, social media, websites, etc.

December 10 - Holiday Card Day

- Send a holiday greeting card to your customers. Post a holiday greeting or New Year wish, quote or sentiment on your Facebook page and blog every day between now and the New Year.

- Post holiday entertaining and party ideas and trivia about holiday traditions on your Facebook page, blog and email newsletter. Solicit/share holiday stories, family traditions and customs.

December 13 - Cookie Cutter Day

- Purchase inexpensive ornaments or branded (personalized to your business) ornaments to give away as client thank-you gifts this month.

- Tell clients why you are not just another "cookie cutter" stylist by highlighting the services at which you excel. Tell customers how your products and services are different and better than others. Talk about what sets your customer service apart. Talk about your personal mission, vision and values and how you make clients lives and the community better.

December 17 - Cut Out Snowflakes Day

- Posts links to snowflake cut-out patterns or decorating ideas on your Facebook page, blog and email newsletter. Solicit customer pictures of snowflakes.

- Use large, cut-out snowflakes to decorate your windows, walls, shelving or to hang from the ceiling to create an indoor winter wonderland in your business.

December 26 - Thank You Note Day

Don't procrastinate, get right on it! Write thank-you notes to vendors, your boss, co-workers, marketing partners, landlord, businesses located near yours and/or any customers who gave you a gift, or to whom you wish to extend a special, personal thank you before the end of the year.

 Facebook　 Twitter　 Blog　 Email/Mail

 December

Sunday	Monday	Tuesday	Wednesday	Thursday	Friday	Saturday
						1
2	3	4 ✉ f t **Send December email newsletter and offers**	5	6 f t **Roof Over Your Head Day**	7	8
9 **Hanukkah Begins**	10 **Holiday Card Day**	11 f t Look ahead! Finalize Jan. 2013 details and plan Feb. and March	12	13 📶 f t **Cookie Cutter Day**	14	15
16	17 **Cut Out Snowflakes Day**	18 ✉ f t Send email: Dec. 'Last Chance!' and Jan 2013 preview	19	20	21 f t **Winter Solstice**	22
23	24 **Christmas Eve**	25 ✉ f t **Christmas Day** Send holiday e-greeting	26 **Thank You Note Day**	27	28 f t	29
30 ✉ f t 31 **New Years Eve** Send holiday e-greeting		Take/break down expired promotions; set up for January		*Great things are not done by impulse, but by a series of small things brought together.* (Vincent Van Gogh)		

score card

Check one box for every communication task completed from the above calendar this month:

week one
☐ ☐ ☐ ☐ ☐

week two
☐ ☐ ☐ ☐ ☐

week three
☐ ☐ ☐ ☐ ☐

week four
☐ ☐ ☐ ☐ ☐

week five
☐ ☐ ☐

_____# of **New Clients**
Up/Down from last month #_____

_____# of **Retail Products** sold
Up/Down from last month #_____

 _____# of Facebook Fans/Friends
Up/Down from last month #_____

 _____# of Twitter Followers
Up/Down from last month #_____

 _____# of Blog Hits/Readers
Up/Down from last month #_____

 _____# of Email Subscribers
Up/Down from last month #_____

_____# of Email Opens (if known)
Up/Down from last month #_____

plan ahead

One class, seminar or webinar you'll attend in the next 2 months:

_____

One technique or technical skill you will improve or master next month:

_____

One thing you resolve to change in your work or personal life next month:

_____

The Next Step: Your Business Plan

For many different reasons, a lot of professional beauty "indies" (independent stylists, estheticians and others) **dream of one day opening up their own business.** You might view this as the next step or **ultimate destination** in your career, you may want to enjoy **greater autonomy,** or you may have a vision of a building **a truly unique salon or spa.**

Whether it's in your immediate future plans or not, there are many good reasons to develop your own professional plan and engage in formal long range planning, annually—regardless of whether you intend to open your own business or not.

You'll need a business plan to attract investors or get funding, grants or bank loans.

You may even need a business plan in order to work with manufacturers or vendors that limit themselves to partnering with select organizations.

Your business plan may help you entice influential industry leaders or key executives to become part of your team.

Following are the components common to **traditional business plans,** and which you should **review annually** as part of your long range planning process:

1. **Executive Summary:** Although listed first, you will probably write this last. The executive summary is just that—a summary of everything in the business plan itself. It should be optimistic and bold, but also realistic. You want potential investors, banks, vendors and your team members to be confident, but you don't want to set people up with false expectations or appear as though you are not grounded in reality.

2. **Vision Statement:** What your organization ultimately aspires to become. Your vision should resonate with customers and employees and make those connected to your business feel proud, excited and that they are part of something bigger than themselves. It is the good that your company will ultimately provide to the world. It explains why you are doing what you are doing and the good you want to achieve through your success.

3. **Mission Statement:** A definition of why you (deserve to) exist. Your mission statement should provide a precise description of what you do and describe the business you are in. Your mission statement tells your employees how their roles help to fulfill the vision. Your mission statement is the route you will follow and/or the means by which you expect to achieve your vision.

4. **Company Description**
   a. The history, present state and future of the company
   b. Description of products and services
   c. Description of current customer demographics

5. **Marketing Plan**
   a. Overview of your Industry as a whole
   b. Identification of target market/s
   c. Analysis of direct and indirect competitors
   d. Your Unique Selling Proposition (USP) or point of difference

6. **Operations and Management:** How your business operates; the departments, your organizational chart including both positions and main responsibilities, description of key team members, annual/seasonal schedules, reporting cycles, etc.

7. **Financial Statements, Financial Plan and Projections**

8. **Appendix of Supporting Documents**

December
Extras

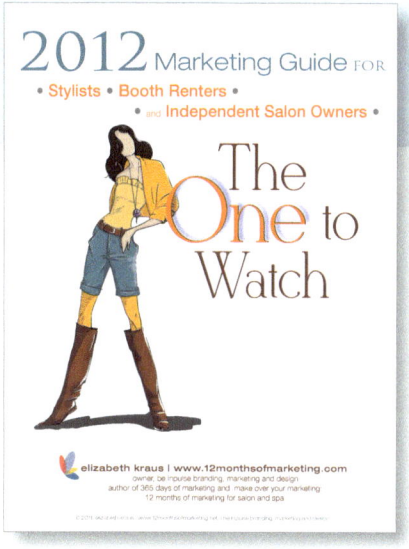

The One to Watch: by elizabeth kraus

owner of Be InPulse branding, marketing and design and author of marketing books including

Make Over Your Marketing: 12 Months of Marketing for Salon and Spa and 365 Days of Marketing (for any small business).

Take the next step in your marketing journey!

More Resources:

Visit www.12monthsofmarketing.com for:
- free newsletters •
- free templates, articles and white papers •
- branded marketing collateral, apparel and promotional items •
- more resources •

Blog: http://www.savvystylist.net

Facebook: www.Facebook.com/elizabethanddan

Google+: Elizabeth Kraus or 12 Months of Marketing for Salon and Spa

LinkedIn: www.linkedin/in/elizabethkraus1

Twitter: www.twitter.com/beinpulse

elizabeth kraus
www.12monthsofmarketing.com
be inpulse branding, marketing and design
author of 365 days of marketing

• learn about marketing—fast! •

• develop your own personal brand for professional success •

• ideas and know-how for social media, email and traditional marketing •

• discover your core strengths and use them to get ahead •

• provide better client service and experiences •

• get referrals and stimulate **real** word-of-mouth marketing •

all in the

2012 Marketing Guide FOR

Stylists • Booth Renters • Independent Salon Owners

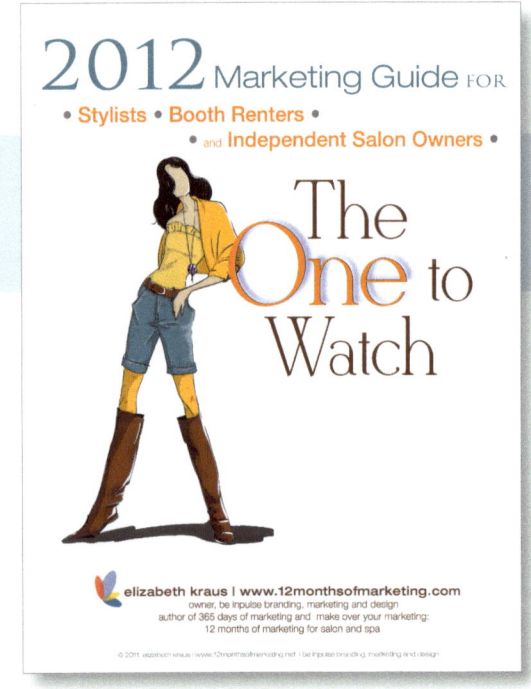

by elizabeth kraus owner of **Be InPulse** branding, marketing and design and author of beauty industry marketing publications including **Make Over Your Marketing: 12 Months of Marketing for Salon and Spa** and the **2012 Salon and Spa Marketing Calendar** as well as 365 Days of Marketing (for any small business) and the 2012 Small Business Marketing Calendar: Little White Marketing Lies—

Take the next step in your marketing journey!

More articles on the blogs at: **http://www.savvystylist.net** and http://365daysofmarketingblog.blogspot.com

Visit **www.12monthsofmarketing.com** for:
- free newsletters, templates, articles and white papers
- branded marketing collateral, apparel and promotional items
- more resources